Praise for For[

This book is a timely reminder to us not that we should forget school but that we should remember to ask ourselves what it is that young people most need to learn today and where best they can do this, both in school and beyond.

Bill Lucas, co-author of *Educating Ruby:*
What Our Children Really Need to Learn

In *Forget School*, Martin Illingworth offers an accurate snapshot of a peculiar and trying phase in human history. By rounding up and extrapolating from the survival techniques of some of those who have managed to hack a living from the carcass of the status quo, Martin provides a timely insight into the novel work practices that may soon constitute the new normal.

Toby Newton, Head of School,
International College Hong Kong

Forget School has the daring and the danger of a protest poster in a totalitarian state – it makes you feel as if you are reading about an educational revolution. Illingworth's voice is at once prophetic and provocative; the voices of his young interviewees authentic and persuasive.

This book should be required reading for all of us who claim an interest in the education of young people in the 21st century.

Mick Connell, PGDE English Tutor,
School of Education, the University of Sheffield

Forget School raises questions that need to be asked about education and schooling before we lose sight of the wonders of learning and the joys of the teaching profession. It reminds us of the privileged position all teachers are in when faced with youngsters desperate to learn and to grow.

Our curriculum offer should teach children to think, form opinions, evaluate, criticise and explore and experiment. Teachers, parents and students ultimately want the same thing: to be happy, confident and successful. In this book Martin Illingworth shines a light on what that could and should be like.

Martin offers a reminder to the profession that we need to be brave and bold, real and authentic and connected to the young people and the world they inhabit. As teachers we wear the badge of 'expert', and Martin prompts us to reconsider what our perception of that role is and should be.

Reading *Forget School* reminds me not only why I became a teacher but why I have continued to love the profession. And 'education' is most definitely only the starting point.

Katy Hodges, SENCO and English teacher

This book is revelatory, inspiring and confirmatory. The voices of young adults reverberate throughout with revelations and sharp insights on their struggles to adapt to the complexities and challenges of a world beyond school that, after years of formal education, they left with a 'currency' they couldn't cash and a lack of 'real world' skills.

Real inspiration in this book comes firstly from the voices of those young people that continue to thrive against the odds and, secondly, from the vision portrayed by Martin Illingworth of an alternative, vibrant, modern educational provision that embraces the modern world, rather that stubbornly ignores it.

Forget School also confirms, with real lucidity, what many within the education world think, and what their instincts as professionals have told them for years – namely that the education system is not fit for purpose and is genuinely damaging to the development of our young people.

John Oswald, Head of Humanities,
Allestree Woodlands School

Why young people are succeeding on their own terms and what schools can do to avoid being left behind

FORGET
SCHOOL

Martin Illingworth

independent
thinking press

First published by

Independent Thinking Press
Crown Buildings, Bancyfelin, Carmarthen, Wales, SA33 5ND, UK
www.independentthinkingpress.com

and

Independent Thinking Press
PO Box 2223, Williston, VT 05495, USA
www.crownhousepublishing.com

Independent Thinking Press is an imprint of Crown House Publishing Ltd.

Extract, pp. 154–155 © TES Reporter (2016). 100 Things You Should Have Done
at School Before the Age of 11 – Chosen by Primary Pupils, TES (22 July).
Available at: https://www.tes.com/news/100-things-you-should-have-done-
school-age-11-chosen-primary-pupils. TES – the online and weekly education
magazine for teachers (www.tes.com/news).

Edited by Ian Gilbert.

British Library Cataloguing-in-Publication Data
A catalogue entry for this book is available from the British Library.

Print ISBN 978-178135313-4
Mobi ISBN 978-178135354-7
ePub ISBN 978-178135355-4
ePDF ISBN 978-178135356-1

LCCN 2019956643

Printed and bound in the UK by
Gomer Press, Llandysul, Ceredigion

How then to put the case for greater quality without appearing to compromise 'standards' in such a toxic political climate? That is the task.

Melissa Benn[1]

A wake-up call to teachers and school leaders, strengthening their arm when it comes to fighting for a better curriculum and also challenging them to do what they can to stretch the curriculum to make it relevant. Teachers can make things happen if they have a will, courage and an understanding of what and why to change.

Ian Gilbert[2]

Kids are perceptive. They know when things aren't just fine and dandy.

Roger Daltrey[3]

1   Melissa Benn, *Life Lessons: The Case for a National Education Service* (London: Verso, 2018), p. 111.
2   Personal correspondence with the author.
3   Roger Daltrey, *My Story: Thanks a Lot Mr Kibblewhite* (London: Blink Publishing, 2018), p. 9.

This book is dedicated to my own grown up children –
Adam, Laurie and Amy – and all the beautiful spirits of
the young people who have contributed their
perspectives on life and energy here.

Also, for Rachel, who made me a room to write in.

Preface

INTRODUCTORY REMARKS

I can't understand why people are frightened of new ideas. I'm frightened of the old ones.

John Cage[1]

As a society we are still sending children to school. We have decided that this is of value and we make all children go. We talk about education – a broad and vague concept. The children go to school and often are not told why it is of value or what they will get from the process.[2] And what do they get? Five live broadcasts a day disappearing into the ether but recorded on parchment with quill. Schooling does not show our children enough of the beauty of their lives now or the potential of what is to come. This is because, as far as I can see, the children are there to serve the school, not the other way around. The school has to compete with the one down the road for a label that says it is a success. This is based on the unpleasant assumption that we want our kids to do better than their kids[3] – a vile basis upon which to educate them all. This is why exams have come to be all-consuming. The examinations should, in reality, be no more than a

---

1 John Cage quoted by Richard Kostelanetz in *Conversing with Cage*, 2nd edn (New York and London: Routledge, 2003), p. 221.
2 Most of the young people who I interviewed in the process of researching this book felt that they would have got more from school if it were clearer what they were personally getting from the experience. Few were actively thinking about what was to be gained.
3 During a September INSET day, I once listened to a head teacher celebrating the fact that his school had 'beaten' another school in the town in the GCSE results. This does not seem to me to be in the spirit of wanting all our children to achieve. Exams as an assessment, of course, need some people to fail to justify their existence.

i

thermometer reading of how things are going with a child's education.

Towering fences supposedly keep the adult world out of the school grounds (which is a huge shame). Perhaps in reality, though, they keep the children in. There is often nowhere to run or to feel the wind on your face at break time, and lunchtimes have been staggered to keep the children apart. The most compliant and middle-class children are on the school council, tinkering with the status quo, whilst the least compliant are flattened in isolation booths.

The task most days is to guess what the teacher wants to hear and then remember it. The teachers just need the children to pass their exams so that they can keep their jobs. The tests examine what they already know and so are of very limited value and the teachers have long since stopped being allowed to write or reinvigorate the curriculum. Children have access to existing knowledge through the phones in their back pockets, but phones are taboo and shunned in school. Most of what is to be remembered turns out to be of no further use. The world has moved on (several times) and schools have been left behind.

Children's suitability for the adult world is decided by the tests that measure the narrowest range of a child's capacities. When children leave school, they have formed lifelong opinions about how clever they are. Most have decided that they are not. Their futures are hugely uncertain, but we continue to tell children that if they work hard and pass their exams then they will get a good job and a happy life.[4]

The government appears to be largely disinterested in schools and schooling. This is part of a wider disinterest in youth at the moment. The ubiquity of the internet means that

---

4   There is a good deal of evidence to suggest that a degree isn't as valued by employers as it once was. See, as a starting point, Liz Burke, University Degrees 'Irrelevant' to Big Employers, *news.com.au* (29 January 2016). Available at: https://www.news.com.au/finance/work/careers/university-degrees-irrelevant-to-big-employers/news-story/8a0340dd2b8e70e35b8ce33 02c8d0cc5.

the government has lost control of information and resorts to an outdated curriculum to assert some kind of control over what citizens are taught to think and know. But the young now have the tools to know better. They need new skills and new ways of thinking. Schools are at a crossroads: respond to the real world of change, challenges and possibilities that face our young, or become irrelevant.

The signs indicating that the young have lost respect for schooling are everywhere. They have learnt the limited value of the curriculum and the associated tests and they are turning their backs on the whole thing. We can't afford to waste their time any longer.

Do you recognise this polemic? Does it ring true with you? Does it make you cross? Let's talk about it.

My purpose here is to get you thinking about the way in which our young people will encounter a whole new set of circumstances as they enter their adult lives and how we might need to change what we offer in schools to help them succeed.

The invention of the printing press created a seismic change in our language and, by extension, in our society. Literacy began to spread and information became more freely available. With greater access to information came new ways of thinking, new ways of being. The limiting factor of this invention, as remains the case with many more recent ones, was the need for physical resources. The printing press required paper. The camera relied on film paper. Sound recordings relied on wax cylinders and vinyl. Now a digital age is upon us and we no longer need physical resources with which to store writing, images and sound – provided we have the increasingly ubiquitous devices which allow us to access them. These things can 'live' in the cloud and be conjured up at any time. The speed of change has accelerated.

The internet and, more specifically, artificial intelligence (AI) are heralding a speed and scope of change of proportions that we cannot easily fathom. We invented machines that at first extended our ability to be safe and informed. Now those machines are becoming cleverer than those who invented them. How we deal with the issues and concerns that this new technology raises, and how we make use of such advances, will be crucial in how humans prosper going forward. The future is always supposed to be some distant time yet to be, but the future has arrived, and we are not yet prepared for it.

Our education system was built in an era when we needed to spread information. Now we have so much information that we are struggling to know how to deal with it all. We still look to measure student achievement by what the pupil 'knows' and by how much they can retain and remember, but new technology has made this approach to learning virtually redundant.[5] We all have the information at our fingertips. What is important now is that we build an educational system that places less value on declarative knowledge (knowing and retaining information) and more on procedural knowledge (the capacity to make use of that information). At the moment, I think that we are failing to properly educate our young, but we seem to be getting away with it because the young are educating themselves through the new technological opportunities that they have. The young are beginning to ignore the generation that went before them, because that generation has shied away from confronting change head-on. In truth, young people have learnt about the tool of communication known as the internet and have mastered its use without any formal instruction or 'education'. But as constant access to the internet becomes commonplace and fewer and fewer people remember a time when it was not a natural part of living, we need to be alert to its hazards. Much can be achieved online, but much can go wrong. These are exciting but dangerous times and we need to support our children to understand their relationship with the world around them.

---

5   And this observation is far from new. See, for example, Murray Wardrop, Learning by Heart Is 'Pointless for Google Generation', *The Telegraph* (2 December 2008). Available at: https://www.telegraph.co.uk/education/primaryeducation/3540852/Learning-by-heart-is-pointless-for-Google-generation.html.

I think one implication of the digital age is that, in thirty or so years, there may well be no physical schools. We will have stopped gathering children of a similar age together to feed them a one-size-fits-all curriculum, regardless of who they are, where they live and their interests. How we measure a child's capacities will also need to change. Examinations are no longer fit for function: we need a new way to support people on their lifelong learning journeys.[6] Just as we no longer rely on physical copies of texts, images and sounds, I suspect we no longer need physical schools. If you think this is crazy talk, consider whether you think that the system we have now will be appropriate in the coming age of automation, artificial intelligence, Blockchain, and virtual and augmented realities.

For those young people who are aspirant and confident enough to take opportunities that present themselves, there are an abundance to be grasped. The expectations of the young are broad: they are the most informed and well-travelled generation ever.[7] Whilst we must acknowledge that the playing field is far from level (something which we'll discuss at numerous points), I believe that the statement 'most informed and well-travelled generation ever' is true for the young at every economic level. Their access to information and resources is unprecedented, and fairly democratic. This changes what young people expect of life. Each generation watches the next changing and adapting according to how they want to live – and my interviewees' generation is moving away from the last (mine) at the most accelerated rate ever seen. The young receive information, ideas and perspectives in all sorts of new forms, most notably, of course, through the

---

6　Toby Baker and Laurie Smith, The Beginning of the End of Exams, *Nesta* (3 December 2018). Available at: https://www.nesta.org.uk/feature/ten-predictions-2019/beginning-end-exams/.

7　Millennials travel more than any other age group and the amount of travelling that they do is increasing. See *The Blue Swan Daily*, Targeting UK Millennials? New Insight Shows They Will Take and Spend More on Leisure Trips During 2019 in Spite of the Clouds Over Brexit (20 March 2019). Available at: https://blueswandaily.com/targeting-uk-millennials-new-insight-shows-they-will-take-and-spend-more-on-leisure-trips-during-2019-in-spite-of-the-clouds-over-brexit/.

internet. This has reshaped how they see themselves and their potential place in the world.

Melissa Benn's eloquent and well-informed *Life Lessons: The Case for a National Education Service* documents the government's failure to deliver an education system that is fit for purpose.[8] Governments' and schools' attempts to be the fonts and gatekeepers of knowledge are over. Schools need to look again at their offer. The young need to network, they need to communicate effectively over digital mediums,[9] they need to manage money and they need to be alert to the world around them. There are new pressures on their mental stability, pressures that diminish the joy of childhood and the sense of readiness – when the time comes – to be a mindful individual and a responsible and caring citizen. If the system does not respond quickly then the young will no longer see any relevance to their schooling. This dissatisfaction is already growing.

Children go to school because they have to. The adult generation has agreed that this is what happens. There follows an assumption that what children receive – their education – is worth having. In listening to my successful young interviewees talking about their lives and their businesses, I am increasingly persuaded that we can no longer assume that the current 'education' on offer in our schools is the best that we can provide. Not even close. One young person who I interviewed as part of my research, a barber, said:

> 'When I left school, I had no idea how much money I needed to make a decent living ... but I knew that plants need sunshine and water to grow.'

8 Benn, *Life Lessons*.
9 Jacob Snelson, The Digital Necessity, *Medium* (4 August 2017). Available at: https://medium.com/digital-society/the-necessity-of-technology-85462f953910.

Think of this. What if going to school were optional? What do you imagine the take-up would be? For those children who choose not to come along, what do you imagine they would give as reasons for non-attendance? Do you think that they would say that they don't want to learn or that they don't want to learn in the way in which school chooses to offer learning? What do you think they would see as relevant and useful to their lives now and in the future? And for those who would still attend, what would they say is useful?

Schools have been left behind because they are operating with a crowd-control mentality. Investment in schools has focused on providing new buildings and on controlling how children conduct themselves in them. Do up your tie, wear your blazer unless you are told you can take it off, stand in line, be in a house system: these things are ephemeral side issues – the structural devices of a school. Little proper attention has been paid to what is taught and its value to the child in school today or to the citizen they will be tomorrow. The way in which our society operates and the values that it hopes to share have changed and are in a cycle of constant further change. What do we tell the children? This is the most important question of them all.

The internet means that access to information has become hugely democratic and knowledge has been taken out of the control of governments and their purveyors of culture: schools. Children can now learn as they choose. They are able to make choices about what and when to learn. They tend to choose on a need-to-know basis and want to learn right here, right now. They like to multi-source, preferring sound and image over print. This is not the model prevalent in schools. There is a growing tension between the ways in which schools teach and the ways in which children want to learn. Alongside this, schools have become a much smaller part of the ecosystem of a child's potential learning. The school curriculum has to compete with wider opportunities to find things out. Unfortunately for teachers, this throws light on the out-of-date curriculum that they are being asked to deliver.[10] When we decry the death of reading ('Kids never read these days', which, by the way, is nonsense. They read loads more than they did when I was at school. Try taking their phones off them and see just how badly they want to read – the issue is that we are reluctant to class consuming messages and online content as 'reading'). What we are really talking about is the downturn in reading – at length – of novels and non-fiction texts. But that old-fashioned means of story-making is now competing with *Fortnite*, and with Facebook, and with *FIFA*, and with films, and with FaceTiming your friends. There are so many choices, so why choose the one that the previous generation is insisting upon?

The dominant model of school education is that of passive, non-participatory reception of old knowledge that is to be remembered and then demonstrated in a test of memory. That is not how the young choose to learn in their own time and it is not how society at large operates. The curriculum is lagging behind culture. Schools become both symptom and cause of low aspiration, of downward pressure on children, causing unhappiness and spreading dis-ease. Children are offered a diet of knowledge retention, remembering facts that go largely unexplained in terms of why they are being learnt or what their use will be.

In choosing to write about what I see as the real crisis in education, I am seeking to support the work of teachers. Teachers remain the only real stable resource in the classroom and their work is as vital as ever. I have been a schoolteacher and educator for a long time and I am frustrated by the ways in which educating children is constantly being taken out of our hands. I am an insider who thinks that we all need a wake-up call and that those best placed to deliver it are our children. We need to listen to what they are telling us about the schooling they have received. Look at the way in which, in recent years, schoolchildren have ignored their teachers and

---

10 Victoria Fenwick, Are We Creating a Generation of Forrest Gumps?, *TES* (2 August 2019). Available at: https://www.tes.com/news/are-we-creating-generation-forrest-gumps.

protested on our streets about climate change.[11] They see more value in a day spent finding their individual and collective voices on the streets than in a day spent in the classroom. I think that many would agree with them.

If things are not right and you stay quiet, then they will never change. Change in our school curriculum will only occur when we insist upon it. Otherwise, our power to insist may very well be taken away because children will no longer afford us the authority to talk to them.

We (by which I mean teachers, leaders, educationalists, etc.) can debate (a generous description of some exchanges) with each other on Twitter and other such forums. Ultimately though, our children will take their education off somewhere safer. If you can't see the sense in the argument I'm putting forward, or you think I am plainly wrong, then at least reading this book will give you the chance to think about what you want for your children's futures. It's okay for you to disagree, but please listen to the young people whose voices fill these pages. They are full of life, full of energy (sometimes a different energy to the one that we require in our classrooms) and I think that they need our help. They need advocates and we are well placed to be those people.

… **don't rely on the adults too much. Most of them mean well, but they just don't understand the world.**

Yuval Noah Harari[12]

The questions being asked, and the issues being addressed, in education today are just too small. In-fights over funding, over types of schools, over local and national control, and

11 Patrick Knox, Youth Climate March: Thousands of Student Climate Change Protesters Descend on Central London in Record-Breaking Turnout, *The Sun* (24 May 2019). Available at: https://www.thesun.co.uk/news/9145737/fridays-for-future-climate-change-protesters-110-countries/.
12 Yuval Noah Harari, *21 Lessons for the 21st Century* (London: Jonathan Cape, 2018), p. 266.

over exam content fail to see the future coming. We need to be pursuing the answers to much bigger questions, such as:

- What should the functions of the curriculum be in the 21st century?
- What subjects/topics (that are not on the syllabus) would young people like to study?
- Are there subjects that we should add to the school curriculum that are not currently taught?
- What skills and proficiencies does society actually need the young to have right now?
- Where are the lines to be drawn between essential and specialised knowledge? For instance (and to start an argument!), to what age (if at all) should you be taught science as a compulsory subject?
- In what ways do we actually use our ability to read today? Does this have an implication for how reading and text is approached in schools?
- What is important and relevant in each subject? What do children need to know in fifteen years' time when they are the new adult population taking our society forward?
- How can we broaden and diversify the curriculum so that everyone feels that the education they receive is about them? (Edexcel have made a start on this with their additions to reading lists for GCSE English.)
- How should we record a child's journey through education?
- It is clear that we need to replace exams, but how do we best 'measure' children's developing capacities?
- How are we going to approach AI and electronic devices so that we get the best possible use from them?
- It's potentially difficult to do, but how are we going to promote confidence and well-being in our school curriculum?

- If there is no level playing field, how will we support those who are disadvantaged?

- In what ways will your pupils be 'richer' when they leave your school? You could ask yourself this question after every lesson if you want a good guide as to whether it was worth doing or not.

- There is a good deal of new research into the brain and, more specifically, into how we learn. How will we train teachers to have a working knowledge of the latest neuroscientific thinking?

Consider where you are as a teacher – and where your department or key stage and school are – in relation to answering some of these questions. The questions around curriculum are big but they need addressing right now. The nature of the help that our young need in understanding who they are and in thinking about the life they want for themselves now and in the future has changed. Children's 'poor' behaviour is symptomatic of the fact that schools are becoming redundant in the learning that they offer – and bickering over other purported causes won't solve the issue. Children's 'poor' behaviour is fundamentally telling us that these children are uncomfortable with the curriculum that they are being offered, not because it is unfamiliar and difficult and they are scared of it – as some would have us believe – but because it is clear that it does not match their needs. Not anymore. We must do something about it.

CONTENTS

Chapter 3: Connections   53

Young people see the value of networking and understand that working together will get them further. Being connected leads to opportunities that you wouldn't get alone and is important as a way of working in what is being described as the 'age of loneliness'. Many are now making global connections and seeing the potential of being a world citizen.

Chapter 4: Money management   67

The young have had to develop an appreciation and a sense of economics that includes investing time and capital in their endeavours: understanding how to budget and how to manage debt are key skills. What role should schools play in developing economic sense in the age when the 1% own half of global wealth? Our children leave school with little idea of how to support themselves or grow financially.

Chapter 5: Happiness and well-being   77

This is a key measurement of success for young people, who can see that mental health and well-being is a choice. Austerity may well have taught the young the value of 'enough', but they still have to plan to be happy or else be swept away by anxiety. Are we able to teach happiness? Is it something that we can equip them to plan for?

Chapter 6: Relationships   89

We all need to maintain a personal life and leisure time that does not get subsumed in the idea that if you're not working then you're not earning – this idea can be a real threat. Being active in maintaining a private life is another key skill for young people to develop.

Chapter 7: Developing talents   95

In the 21st century and beyond, we are all going to have to keep reinventing ourselves as how we live changes. The opportunity to learn online for free and on demand is shifting how and when we really learn. We are going to have to re-define the scope of what an education means. We are going to have to learn throughout our lives because of the rate of change in modern society. How can we make the schooling that the young receive become the first step of their journey through lifelong education, and not just something they endure to pass exams and then forget?

Chapter 8: Making decisions and being creative   109

What's important here is understanding that you will make mistakes and that living with uncertainty is going to need some smart thinking. There is a rise in the perceived value of 'soft skills' and practical, instantaneous learning over that which can be inferred from a university degree. Being able to make decisions is a key skill in moving forward; being creative could well be the making of you.

Chapter 9: Ethics   117

Young people are increasingly alert to the need to look after their planet and the people on it. Vegetarians, vegans, sustainable living advocates and climate change protesters are the new black! Treating each other with respect and doing what's right are the justifications for young people's moral standpoints.

Chapter 10: 'Qualifications'   123

The young continue to want to learn, but they have become weary and suspicious of the modes by which they are being assessed and becoming qualified. This is changing how they perceive 'being qualified' for a job. The exam system is losing its authority in the eyes of the young. This mistrust will be the end of it.

Chapter 11: Discrimination   135

Here there is some discussion of the barriers that young people are facing in developing their portfolios. From a broader perspective, they suffer from having little chance of living as adults with the debts that they are accruing. There are also a number of everyday cruelties that the young have to face.

Chapter 12: What do children need to know in fifteen years' time?

A truly disempowering question for the teacher who thinks that their job is done if they just trust that the curriculum is worth offering as is. How well will the curriculum that you offer today serve those young people in the days and years to come? Do we facilitate our teachers in staying up to date with their curriculum knowledge?

Chapter 13: What can schools do right now to avoid being left behind?

Whilst we wait for the government's educational insights to catch up with the needs and challenges of the real world, here are some things that we can be doing in our classrooms, with our curriculum and with our intentions.

Chapter 14: 'Final decisions are made in silent rooms'

Some final thoughts. I would say that the single most important factor that will impact on a child's academic success is going to be effort. Can we offer an education that is worth the effort? Can we offer an education which makes clear what that effort will amount to in terms of its value?

An afterthought

References and reading list

A selection of some wonderfully illuminating reading material that will support you in thinking about your teaching and the importance of what you are doing in the classroom.

Index

an explanation

'My advice? Forget school. No really, forget it. I've learnt so much since I left and forgotten most of what I learnt then …'

I spent much of the year and a half that led up to me writing this book interviewing young people who I consider to be 'successful'. In writing up my findings, I hope to investigate the ways in which the young are making a future for themselves despite the, sometimes, poor preparation that schooling is offering them. The perspectives and arguments outlined in these pages are theirs. I have chosen to write about the most significant and high-frequency concerns and hopes that they expressed. In doing this, I hope that I have given them a voice that we can listen to and so that we can begin to address the issue of providing an education worthy of the name. How to provide an education worth having is a subject that we are going to have to keep returning to time and again in the coming years. Our world changes so fast. The way in which we educate our children must keep pace.

This book will in part consider how the young measure their own success. It is the young themselves that I think offer us hope. Despite the hurdles in their way, young people continue to thrive, continue to be hopeful and continue to try to make sense where none seems to be. We need to reward their energy and optimism with an education of hope.

Since we have to live with uncertainty, only those who are certain (should) leave the room before the discussion can become adult.

Christopher Hitchens[1]

Throughout the book I use the expression 'the young' as a collective term for my interviewees and their contemporaries. These young people are all aged between 20 and 30. They come from many walks of life and different social classes, and are finding their ways across various different employment sectors. They work in the fields of accountancy, acting, architecture, aviation, banking, building trades, caregiving, catering, charity, fashion, film, graphic design, hairdressing, law, medicine, music, personal training, photography, product design, retail, tailoring, theatre and wedding design. Some of the interviews lasted well over an hour; others were more fleeting.

All of these young people are working for themselves or are in the process of moving from paid employment to self-employment. Being in paid positions working for someone else is not their main career aspiration. Estimates for August to October 2019 suggest that there were a record 4.96 million self-employed people in the UK, which represents a rise of 182,000 from the previous year.[2] That might be because the alternative is a zero-hours contract or a job that means they are living on the breadline, or it might be because they have found the courage and desire to 'make it' on their own. Surely one of the core functions of our schools must be to support young people to have the presence of mind to rise to the challenge of the 21st-century marketplace in a post-truth

1 Quoted in Richard Dawkins, Daniel C. Dennett, Sam Harris and Christopher Hitchens, *The Four Horsemen: The Discussion that Sparked an Atheist Revolution* (London: Bantam Press, 2019), p. 77.
2 Office for National Statistics, Employment in the UK: December 2019 [statistical bulletin] (17 December 2019). Available at: https://www.ons.gov.uk/employmentandlabourmarket/peopleinwork/employmentandemployeetypes/bulletins/employmentintheuk/december2019.

world with a sense of their own capacity and know-how. We live in uncertain times. Our young people will face many challenges in their adult lives. Schooling must be, in part, a preparation for this. We must also support them to deal with the fact that society is going to keep reinventing itself as the possibilities change over and over again. The world is becoming both bigger (we can travel further, faster and cheaper than ever before) and smaller (we are connected with people all around the world) at the same time. The world is becoming more intimate, and with this new connectedness comes a rising sense of expectation about what is possible. The young have a very different set of expectations of 'normal' to the previous generation.

And what a refreshing experience it is to talk to young people who are so driven and motivated to make a life that suits and sustains them. I asked all kinds of questions (a list of the most frequent ones follows), but at its core the interview that I conducted sought their views on how they had built their success and on the ways in which their schooling was useful – and, of course, the ways in which it had been a hindrance. In the following pages I offer you the voices of these young people and also the patterns of answers that I have been able to discern, which throw light on what sort of an education they could have done with and what might suit those children who are in school now. In tone, the general range of perceptions ran from those for whom school was fine (if a little dull) to those who remain in recovery.

The voice of this text is my own, but it seeks to amplify a further voice: a composite of the voices of the young people who I interviewed. It is my summing up of the patterns and ideas that were prevalent in the responses that I was offered, which I hope honestly and accurately reflects their feelings and aspirations. These young people are individuals but quite a lot of the time they spoke with one voice and, as time went on, I kept hearing recurring concerns and repeated thoughts about their lives and their education. These themes have been distilled into the chapters that follow.

'School did not give me an honest account of just how big knowledge is ... how unknowable and how illusive ... and it didn't help me find things out.'

Interspersed into the text are direct quotes from individual interviewees. Sometimes when people are talking to you, certain ideas and phrases stand out in capturing the essence of what is being said.

'When I think about all the questions I answered in my GCSE exams – across all the subjects (laughs) ... it's a right ragbag bunch of silliness.'

Voices are important. Having a voice is important. Being allowed a platform from which to speak, to a forum who will listen, is important. Being listened to is one of those things that promotes self-esteem and confidence. Our instinct is perhaps to listen to the voices of experience and to consult the voices of the past: our elders and our betters. People with power are also influential. Increasingly though, the young are talking amongst themselves. Our young can more easily communicate between themselves, as the internet has allowed access to a vast pool of potential connections.

Paul Dolan suggests that we listen to some people more than others.[3] Those who get listened to the most tend to have three things that we look for, whether we do that consciously or subconsciously. Firstly, they can be trusted. Secondly, we see them as experts. (Perhaps the trust grows from the expertise or maybe the expertise develops trust.) Thirdly, we tend to listen to those who are like us. We tend to pay attention to those who might well reflect back what we already know or what we want to believe in. This is why big data has become

3 Paul Dolan, *Happiness by Design: Finding Pleasure and Purpose in Everyday Life* (London: Penguin, 2014).

such an important tool for those trying to persuade us to buy or to agree. We trust and believe in those people who are like us. Big data can tell what your beliefs are and reflect them back to you for a whole range of purposes: swaying the way you vote and making you buy things would be two good examples.

But who is listening to the voices of the young these days? As the lights fell on the main stage of Barn on the Farm in 2017, and the festivalgoers trooped off to their tents, the air rang from the whole festival ground with the strains of 'Oh, Jeremy Corbyn'. Something important was stirring in Great Britain, born of the frustrations of the young who were being excluded from joining the mainstream of adult life because they couldn't get a mortgage or more than a zero-hours contract, and austerity was biting them at every turn.

In December 2019, the Conservative government won the general election with a strong majority. However, the polls show that if just the 18–24 age group was voting then the outcome would have been very different. Labour polled 56% of the vote with this age group whilst the Tories achieved just 21%.[4] This is stark confirmation that the generation gap is yawning wide; that the adult world is cold to our young. Clearly, making use of Paul Dolan's list of tendencies, the young do not trust the government, do not see them as capable and certainly don't see themselves belonging to that set of values.

---

4   See Adam McDonnell and Chris Curtis, How Britain Voted in the 2019 General Election, YouGov (17 December 2019). Available at: https://yougov. co.uk/topics/politics/articles-reports/2019/12/17/how-britain-voted-2019-general-election.

The questions

I conducted all the interviews myself, in all kinds of settings: from university interview rooms to coffee houses and the beer gardens of pubs. Whilst the questions followed a similar format, they also diverted off into conversations and follow-up questions that pursued what I considered to be interesting sidetracks. As a member of one generation exploring the understandings, thoughts and feelings of another, you sometimes have to follow their lead. In fact, most of the time!

I had three overarching questions:

- What was good about school?
- What was bad about school?
- What have you had to learn for yourself?

Then in pursuing recurring patterns of response, I variously asked:

- In what ways was school useful in preparing you for the work you do now?
- Why are you self-employed?
- How creative would you say you are?
- What specifically do you want to achieve?
- How do you measure success?
- On a scale of 1 to 10, where are you now in being a success?
- What is your strongest/main reason for wanting to achieve this success?
- Are there any sacrifices that you are making?
- What knowledge, skills or experiences are supporting you?
- Is there anything that is blocking your way to success?

- Do you think you will always be doing the work that you do now?
- Are there ways in which your industry is changing (and will you have to change)?
- What concerns do you have?
- From where/whom do you normally seek advice?
- Are you politically interested/active?
- Which contemporary issues are important to you?
- Are there any particular ethical decisions that you make in your work?
- Where do you get your work from?
- At what age did you feel like an adult?
- If school were optional, what reasons would you have had to go?
- How do you feel about the exam results that you have achieved?
- What uses have you put your exam results to?
- What skills/attributes/qualifications do you look for in prospective employees?
- What fulfils you/makes you feel alive?

Chapter 1

CONFIDENCE

'In my business, in my line of work, you are always trying to stand out. I think I spent a lot of my time at school trying to blend in.'

A theme that came up time and again in my interviews was that of confidence: the overriding importance of having it and the debilitating effects of lacking it. I have placed it as the first of the themed chapters because it was highlighted by my interviewees as being very important, and the main thing that their schooling had not provided them with. The criticism was usually not about the way that the teachers were with them as pupils. Rather, it was about not having learnt about how to be comfortable in new and challenging situations. This was perhaps the life skill that most felt that they had to learn for themselves after they left school. This is, I think, a real failing of the current school system. We need to look at the skill of being confident and work out how to teach it explicitly. Confidence and self-belief are surely foundational building blocks for success and achievement. We can all recognise the child who sits quietly in the corner during lessons, delivering written work well above curricular expectations but never speaking. What is our responsibility there?

'At school there was always this definiteness about knowledge that turns out to just not be true. Everything always seemed so important and I felt so small … unimportant in comparison.'

Most of the young agree that you don't get opportunities to learn about and develop confidence in school. School is where they learnt things that don't seem to have a lot to do with their lives. Furthermore, it was not really made clear what school had to do with the real world around them. I wonder if we pay enough attention to telling the pupils in our classrooms what the value of them being there might be. What are the skills, knowledge or new perspectives that are being gained in today's lesson and what are the applications of that learning in the real world outside the school gates? Can you answer these questions about your own classroom? If you can, do you spend time making sure that your pupils know the answers too? In listening to them talk about this subject, it seems that the young feel that they came out of school with a lot to learn about what's really going on. The perception is that this lack of 'real' knowledge can seriously knock your confidence when it turns out that you don't really know anything.

How the young perceive their value and their ability to join in successfully with the world around them are significant factors in how their life chances will develop. Being confident means having the strength and courage to make healthy choices, to accept risks and be able to manage setbacks. More and more young people are choosing or having to go out into the world of work on their own. They are entrepreneurial, open for business. As self-employment continues to become a larger and larger part of the job market, young people increasingly have to learn that they have agency and that they can work autonomously. This mindset will come from their own confidence in their abilities. However, it is also reliant on an adult world that sends them positive messages about who and what they are. For instance, the reaction from some quarters about including LGBT topics as part of sex and relationships education is problematic. If we think that children shouldn't learn about homosexuality, for instance, are we saying that it's not okay to be gay? Surely it would be better to let our young people know that non-heterosexuality is not really a thing of any great remark: it's 'normal'. That attitude would move us further away from the abhorrence of homophobic and transphobic bullying. Young people need to feel confident in themselves, and how their identities will be met, in order to present themselves and their ideas clearly and persuasively.

Stepping out into the adult world, whether that is the world of work or university, is a scary step. Presenting yourself and your ideas, and believing that you will be taken seriously, is also a challenge that will have to be faced by all those who want to make it on their own. Whether you are turning up as a young 'apprentice face' in a large company or setting yourself up as a freelancer in an established field of work, you need to believe that you are going to be able to do it.

The young also need to feel comfortable with the ways in which they are making contact and pursuing opportunities. The mediums through which our young communicate are changing rapidly. Communication still encompasses physical meetings, but more and more often the setting for business is online. Young people need to be able to present themselves effectively across a whole range of platforms. This will also mean learning how to make the best use of these different environments.

'If you are going to be heard, you have to speak.'

I think we can all agree that the way in which the young see jobs and making a living has changed since their parents' generation. The whole idea of work has moved away from single occupation careers – just a means to pay the bills – to a far healthier view of your working life as a way in which you are able to express yourself.

The young have a better starting point than their elders did, with all the access that they have to the wider world. Their mothers and fathers might well say to them – as my interviewees reported that their parents had – that when they were at school you were sold the idea that when you left you decided what you wanted to be, then a careers officer would deem whether that was a possibility. The idea that society sold you was that you would be doing that job until you retired. You need to get a stable job and stick at it! Are you, as a teacher, still peddling this idea?

This next generation does not see this path extending in front of them. If you go to school now, you should expect to take on a number of jobs and you will need to adapt and change constantly throughout your working life. Some of the jobs you might do have yet to be invented. Some that already exist will change beyond all recognition because of technology and society's demands. Some of the jobs and professions that our children might aspire to will be gone by the time they leave school. This poses a real need for schools to acknowledge the shifting nature of the job market and prepare children appropriately. Are you and your colleagues well-versed in these shifts? Are the changes in the skills that we require of our workers reflected in the curriculum design that you offer? How does your numeracy provision take into account the way in which the world is changing?

'University was a doss ... it wasn't proactive enough and it was beginning to have an impact on my mental health. I just couldn't see the point ... so I quit.'

Schools generally still offer the idea of lifelong employment in a single career as a viable possibility and, indeed, the norm. The importance of job security and knowing who you are going to be seems to give schools authority to speak on behalf of the adult world, but that is no longer the case. 'What are you going to become?' used to be a valid question that might shape a useful schooling for you. The idea of building a 'stable identity', which was always a building block of past educational offerings, is not going to be suitable in the future. The advice about lifelong careers traditionally delivered by a careers officer is defunct. Today's young people are going to have to reinvent themselves many times over. This is going to take huge courage and adaptability alongside emotional strength. Well-being is going to be constantly challenged. Some people will get left behind if they follow the old model of sticking to one job or career for a lifetime. You just can't rely on that job always being there. You are going to need a range of skills and a willingness to adapt if you are going to keep your options open wide enough.

The Organisation for Economic Co-operation and Development (OECD) has estimated that over the coming twenty years or so, '14 percent of jobs are at high risk of being fully automated, while another 32 percent at risk of significant change'.[1] This will require some people to retrain entirely and some to develop their skills as their job changes. This will require self-confidence and the knowledge that you are able to meet the challenge of learning, unlearning and relearning. This is an unfamiliar process in our schools.

As I mentioned, most of the young people who I interviewed had moved from salaried roles (that might once have supposed to be 'for life') to using any paid employment as a means of funding what they really want to do. Making use of a contracted job (or several) whilst you get your freelance work up and running is also an increasingly frequent model.

Look at the rise of the 'slashie' phenomenon in Britain. A slashie is someone who works more than one job at a time. Young workers in particular are embracing the idea of holding multiple roles. This was initially born of necessity for those who needed to work more than one job to make ends meet, but the young have put a more positive spin on this situation. Diversifying your work and career choices is seen as a way of making money to support your interests and also giving

---

1   Reported in *Study International*, How Can Schools Prepare Students for the Fourth Industrial Revolution? (31 May 2019). Available at: https://www.studyinternational.com/news/how-can-schools-prepare-students-for-the-fourth-industrial-revolution/.

yourself the chance to hit 'lucky' in more than one area. Anyway, why should you confine your working life to one of your interests when you may have a number that you'd like to pursue? Employers are offering shorter and shorter contracts, and that's if they offer a contract at all, which has also forced the young into thinking about their plan B – and building a backup plan into their perceptions of working life.

'The money's decent but you never know when the work will dry up, so I can't commit full-time.'

Another recurrent theme surrounding confidence was conveyed by the interviewees who told me, 'I can do better than that.' Young people say that they are not afraid of hard work and are prepared to put in a good deal of time and energy. This has driven many of my interviewees to seek out ways of starting up business ventures for themselves.

'I mean c'mon ... they were making these designs that were so poor ... so I added in my ideas and they liked them and then they just took them! I wasn't getting any credit and I wasn't getting any of the profit from the design work ... like, how long are you going to put up with that ... it's like stealing. It's part of the reason I left really. I knew I could do it better and hopefully get rewarded for it ... putting the profits in my pocket instead of theirs.'

Why work for someone else and pour your efforts into their pockets, particularly when you feel that they are not putting in the same level of effort, skill and creativity? The key here is confidence. Do you have the confidence to try to break out on your own? You have to believe that you can find a way to get up and running, get the help you need and just go for it.

It's called agency – believing that you are in control, believing that there is another way. The fact that the model of a job for life has been eroded has had at least one positive impact, in that the young are more able to commit to an endeavour that they are not certain will succeed. They are more likely to give something a go in the knowledge that you can always do something else if it all goes wrong. When I listen to teachers talking to children about their futures, more often than not the discussion is about becoming an employee. It is rare to hear talk of self-employment. I suppose the perception is that the pupils are young and joining the adult world on the bottom rung, so it would be safer and easier for them to fit into existing employment structures.

> 'Confidence is the main thing. You have to have it and that's hard. In school, I guess it depends on how you got through the lessons. If you never spoke up, then you probably find it hard to communicate effectively now. But if you believe in your project, in yourself, then confidence can grow. You get better at things. People give you praise and it feels good.'

Due, in a large part, to the internet, the generation gap is as wide as it has ever been. My interviewees very rarely sought advice from their elders on account of the perception that older people have a lack of knowledge and experience of contemporary trends and current practices. This distance, this lack of contact, is growing. And whether they are right or wrong on this point, their unwillingness to ask for help leaves them to fend for themselves. Setting themselves up on their own is going to take a good deal of self-confidence. But they can be a lively bunch – some would stay stubborn – who are prepared to muddle through and try things out, often at the expense of asking someone older who has got more experience and would probably be able to help them achieve their goal much more quickly!

The young don't watch much television. They certainly don't watch the television news and they tend to get their information about the world through social media platforms and podcasts. The majority of my interviewees watched between zero and three hours of television a week. Most said that they had not watched any BBC or ITV news for over a month. They are cutting themselves adrift from what their parents would consider the normal news outlets. In our post-truth world, young people, or at least the ones I spoke to, do not trust the BBC, thinking that it has a condescending way of 'reporting' the news and then telling everyone what to think about that news.

'Have you noticed the media brainwash? You get the news first thing in the morning and then last thing at night ... it's a trick ...'

Whilst I detected a good deal of respect for the idea of an 'expert', it was certainly true that the experts who the young were talking about were much younger than I'd expected. It seemed to me that their admiration was reserved for their peers who are doing well or who have a 'real talent'. When the young want to learn something, they go to the web to watch video tutorials. On the whole, they choose to learn what they want to know and when they need to know, a somewhat alien model to schools. The curriculum tends to slow down the rate of learning. Things will be important in next week's/month's/year's test. This is not how young people learn in their life outside school. It is also not how the adult world of work learns.

One feature of schoolwork that was considered to have been useful was that of being made to talk. Note the use of the word 'made'. Lots of children are uncomfortable at the thought of talking to their peers during a lesson. It presents the possibility of being wrong or giving away something about yourself in a public forum. Talk can be about showing your frailties and sharing your personality, which can be daunting. However, the young people who I interviewed were expressly able to see the value of talk and, in particular, of giving presentations. Talking in formal situations was one of the activities that was best regarded by my interviewees. Best regarded because the activity itself played a role in developing confidence but also because the skill of oracy had subsequently been useful in adult life.

'At school I really enjoyed doing presentations. Speaking to adults, like when I did my report back from our Africa project, has stayed with me.'

There was more of this sort of activity identified in primary school and in the sixth form. GCSEs were perceived as being all about analysing other people's stuff. There weren't as many opportunities to present then. However, talk for a purpose was well-regarded. Actually having a meaningful audience supports children to do their best – to be at their best when presenting ideas, thoughts and arguments.

'I still remember giving a presentation to some employers during Year 10. It works best for building your confidence when there is a real audience. It makes the talk seem more important. You feel like you have achieved something worthwhile.'

Similarly, working with peers was viewed as time well-spent in school. Group work was well-regarded. There was an honesty about the amount of 'off-topic' chat but also the thought that this is natural when working. There was the general opinion that:

'Teachers think that you're not always focused and doing what you should be when you do group work. Plenty of truth in that, but it is good just to work with people you wouldn't normally interact with. It's interesting to find out that not everyone thinks like you and your friends do.'

There is real merit, regardless of topic, in just seeing how other people operate: how they think, how they express themselves and how they interact. Knowing about how people will respond to situations and proposals can be crucial to being successful in business and in your wider life. Working for yourself, and figuring things out by yourself, is okay, but it isn't always realistic: that's not how we are going to work most of the time out in the real world. In his foreword to Sugata Mitra's *Beyond the Hole in the Wall*, Nicholas Negroponte describes the way in which we segregate children into age groups as a 'bad idea'.[2] Do younger and older people work together in the adult workplace? Yes, they do.

Networking is hugely important and young people need to be prepared to join in. Where are the opportunities in your curriculum to encourage their confidence to speak up? Can we highlight that part of the desired outcome of the work that we do in class is about developing the confidence to interact? Whilst you are often encouraged to list curricular learning objectives on your whiteboard, what is to stop you including developing confidence as an explicit objective as well?

2   Sugata Mitra, *Beyond the Hole in the Wall* [Kindle edition] (TED Books, 2012), loc. 41.

'Sometimes I think that being creative is a lot about believing in yourself. Garden design is so subjective ... you have to believe that you have got something to offer.'

Being a confident person was mentioned many times in my interviews as an achievement. Confidence, perhaps where it is at a premium, is much respected by our young people. The modern era has often been described as the age of loneliness.[3] Loneliness has a devastating impact upon well-being and physical health. I think the young see confidence as one safeguard against being lonely: a tool with which to attract the attention of others and to bolster the perception that others have of them.

'When I think about success, I would say that becoming a confident person is right up there. It is really satisfying to be able to talk to folk and see that they believe in you ... that they trust you. That has really driven me on.'

And sometimes you just have to know your self-worth!

'I am not kidding, there isn't one person in that office who can design even a basic webpage ... they needed me big style ... and now I'm gone, they'd better get a replacement sharpish or they'll be in trouble. I was making a right contribution.'

3 George Monbiot, The Age of Loneliness Is Killing Us, The Guardian (14 October 2014). Available at: https://www.theguardian.com/commentisfree/2014/oct/14/age-of-loneliness-killing-us.

However, confidence can be hard to find within you. We need to help our pupils develop the belief that what they say will be respected and is worth listening to. They must not be afraid to make mistakes. In fact, they need to appreciate the value of mistakes to their learning. We need to create classroom environments in which it is okay to be wrong, it is okay to be thoughtful and it is okay not to know.

'I hated waiting for my turn to speak at school. I could see it coming ... the teacher looking for those people who haven't spoken yet ... I could feel my body tighten.'

Whenever you are faced with a class of thirty people, it is important to remember that they are not one lot of thirty; they are thirty lots of one. Those ones are not equally equipped to deal with talking in front of their peers. They have not all developed the capacity to negotiate, to listen or to have opinions. In the homes of some children there is little opportunity to feel confident. Their lives are full of discord and argument rather than discussion and positive reinforcement. We shouldn't necessarily make judgements about which of our children suffer in this way, but we must be clear that they are in our classes. Those young people in particular need our support.

'Your confidence grows when you know more about the business and you feel your way forward. Suddenly things make sense.'

Working towards an understanding that knowledge and know-how don't always come immediately helps to develop a sense of proportion and the resilience to keep going when you can't at first see a way forward. In schools, by contrast, most lessons seem to be about looking for the shortest route to the right answer, without deviation and without mistakes. This is not a healthy model, nor is it good preparation for the real world.

'Not believing in myself has held me back. It takes time to become confident and I don't even think that being confident is a fixed thing or that you can be equally confident about everything.'

When you are running your own business, you need to develop a sense of your own agency – to believe that you can do things and that you can make decisions. However, your decisions will not always be respected or agreed upon. This can heap pressure on you and have an impact on your confidence. My interviewees demonstrated a good deal of anxiety about whether they were up to the job. This had caused a good deal of sleepless nights for most and emotional trauma for some.

Older generations can tend to laugh at the idea of 'millennial burnout' but I think we all have a little of it these days. Especially for the self-employed, it is hard to be 'off duty'. Judging from my interviews, the young are pretty much always at work. They are always contactable. They are quick to accept responsibility for this 'failing' and say that it is their fault, but they still feel 'out of it' if they switch off their phones. But then what are you to do? The jobs are predominantly online. If you are not online, then the jobs are going to go elsewhere. You have to be able to respond quickly. You need a presence that suggests that you will be worth dealing with, that you'll be reliable. Websites and certain social media channels now report how quickly you are likely to respond. You need to work those numbers to demonstrate your trustworthiness and competence.

'Most of the time I am sure that I wouldn't miss anything but, even so, you can't take the chance of missing out on something.'

This constant pressure can have a really negative impact on young people. The need to be somewhere else can take over all kinds of situations and spoil their attempts to have a healthy social and personal life. It dampens their confidence because it suggests that they are always chasing work rather than people coming to them.

'I also find it really hard to say no to work. Sometimes though, you just have to decide that you won't take something on. There is a skill to recognising when you should say no.'

Are schools good at teaching time management? I can think of the school homework planner as one tool that they provide, but past that there seems to me to be very little support. Managing time and making sure that you are not always at work is a constant challenge for the young people who I interviewed. If schoolwork were more project-based, would this demand that pupils have to make decisions about what is to be done when, setting deadlines and thinking about longer term goals?

Sometimes happily, the young are able to say no, and they offered me a number of reasons why. Listen to the positivity and reflectiveness in the following voices:

'I know my own limitations; I know when I have yet to develop a skill or a capacity to do a job and that I am not fully confident because of that.'

'Sometimes it will be an ethical decision. Some jobs just go against how I feel things should be done and against the way I see the world.'

'Money can be a big consideration. Sometimes I choose not to take up work because I'm not being fairly remunerated for my skills, time and the work I produce.'

'A poor client relationship will also stop me. If I am not being allowed to do the job the way that I want to, or that I can put my name to, because of the ways that the client acts or takes over, then I just won't get involved.'

'A tough one is time limitations; being honest enough with yourself when you don't physically have the time to do a job. This can be tough when it feels like you know you are turning down paid work.'

The young appreciate the need to keep developing their acumen within any occupation but were generally less prepared for the prospect of their job becoming obsolete. It's hard to know or see ahead to what's coming, which can really have an impact on confidence. It can also impact upon the level of commitment that you feel you can give to a job/profession.

'I am doing this work because I love it. I am confident that people will always need a [delete as applicable] personal trainer/wedding designer/photographer/graphic designer/coffee house manager/engineer/musician …'

But the doubts can creep in. Can we help the young to see adversity as a challenge, to see a problem as an opportunity? Where is the problematised curriculum? When do children get to solve questions without definite answers in your lessons? Questions without any answer? A problematised curriculum with open-ended questions will more accurately reflect the sorts of work that the coming years will bring. As mentioned elsewhere, jobs that can be measured and quantified (i.e. with right and definite answers) will largely become obsolete in the not too distant future.

'It takes a lot of confidence to keep investing when you're never quite sure about the market ... about what people want ... there are a lot of what-ifs.'

'I get most of my work through the net and through word of mouth. It can be hard to stay confident that there is going to be a constant flow of work. I tend to stay online most of the time just in case I miss any opportunities because I don't get back to people quickly enough.'

One of the questions that I asked was, 'At what age did you feel like an adult?' To a certain extent, I think that this question is about confidence; it looks for a degree of readiness. It is asking about how prepared people feel to be their own person. There were some interesting answers to this question. Most young people felt that they became 'adult' after they left school and in the main because they had left home, typically to move to university. Going to university is increasingly one of the only viable ways for a young adult to 'leave' home. A mortgage is largely out of the question and rents are high when you are starting out. Without the impetus of going to university, many young people would otherwise continue to live at home whilst they try to establish a career.

'It was certainly not whilst I was at school, not even in the sixth form. I think it was when I left my childhood home. Going to university and moving away from home was quite a test of my confidence.'

'I really wasn't prepared for being my own person, if you like, rather than being a family member in a family home. We did talk about it a bit in sixth form, but before you leave home you can't know how it will feel.'

Time and again my interviewees said that they did not get their self-belief from school. For me, this is one of the most disappointing and upsetting things to be told about their experience of schooling. Surely, this has to be a priority for our education system. We should certainly aim to build opportunities to develop confidence and self-esteem into the work that we ask pupils to undertake. A lack of confidence is a truly debilitating aspect of personality in a time that is so uncertain. If young people are to feel confident, schools need to build in them a repertoire of skills that will serve them well once they reach the adult world of work.

'School makes you feel not clever ... if you know what I mean.'

'School made me feel inadequate really ... there is a pressure to achieve all the time because you are supposed to be bright.'

There are also those pupils who are deemed by the school system not to be bright. Bottom-set kids who know they are bottom-set and add that to the way they feel about themselves. It is hard to be confident when your inadequacies are being made plain every day in the way in which you are spoken to and spoken about. We need to pay attention to building confidence in these 'weak' students. They need to hear what they are good at and need to be spoken to in positive ways about planning for the future. We need to focus on the 'can do'. Otherwise we are offering them the material to write an anti-CV when they leave school.

Our teaching assistants (TAs) are a vital part of how schools operate because they spend their time with, and bring their understanding of, the most vulnerable individuals in our school communities. I spoke with a TA recently who told me about the Year 7 girl who she supports. This 11-year-old has two main problems: she has poor literacy and she doesn't have any friends. She sits by herself at the back of the class in most lessons. She has confided in her TA that the reason why she doesn't talk much is because she waits for other people to talk to her because she feels like she is pushing people if she begins a conversation. She also told her TA that she has created an imaginary person who she becomes and that she has imaginary friends. This represents a crisis of confidence. It is also the main issue that this child needs to overcome before she can prosper in other aspects of her studies. As teachers, we need to understand those times when confidence holds the key to learning; this is certainly one of those times. This story broke my heart but TAs, I am sure, must have their hearts broken every single day.

We need to put confidence as an aim at the very heart of the curriculum. We need to make it an explicitly teachable part of what we do. Curriculum content needs to be reviewed for opportunities to support children to develop their senses of agency and autonomy. It is not good enough to say that we already do that. It is clear from these young voices that they did not learn to be confident in school. We need to be explicit with the pupils about how we learn and about the fact that some learning involves the development of confidence. With the development of technological means for writing, how we communicate is bound to change in the coming years. We need to keep upgrading how we teach communication. Our children need, more than ever, training in speaking and listening, in group work that will support networking in adult life, and in understanding that they have a voice and that they must use it.

> 'I have really seen my confidence grow this last year. I have realised that I can make a difference to how well the coffee house does with the way I am ... that's a real success for me.'

How can you revise the curriculum so that confidence-building is at the heart of what you cover and what you do? After all, confident learners make for confident exam-doers in the short term (if that is your worry!).

'Allow yourself to make mistakes,
Know which ones to keep'[4]

Being confident allows the young to recognise that time is a commodity which they can invest. It will give them the push to grind out a future. Hard work will pay off, but they need to believe that they are going to be able to do it. Confidence is a key factor in making good choices and in accepting that you will make mistakes.

> 'Struggling is not failing ... not for me anyway ... it is an invitation to keep going.'

It can be difficult because past wisdom and knowledge is becoming a less reliable guide for our young people. Most

---

4   Rhythmical Mike, spoken word artist, and acclaimed YouTube and Instagram performer.

'timeless' wisdom seems to be going out of date or is unheeded. Young people think that they would be better looking forward rather than backwards to understand just which way the wind is blowing. Confidence lies forward and it's within reach.

You often hear people say that they worry about having a child because they wouldn't want to bring new life into our world. I say that we should bring children into our world, and let them change it. I agree with James Lovelock, who, aged 100, had this to say:

A child is not born with an immediate ability to understand the environment. It takes many months before it senses the world and years before it can change it.[5]

---

5 James Lovelock, *Novacene: The Coming Age of Hyperintelligence* (London: Allen Lane, 2019), p. 119.

Chapter 2
DIGITAL PROFICIENCY

'You've got to watch yourself on the internet ... really ... there are too many scams and too many things that are too good to be true.'

This is, of course, the big game changer. Technological innovation is in large part why schools need to adapt to stay relevant.[1] Education can't just stay the way it is now. Every young person nowadays has grown up with the internet, with laptops, tablets and smartphones. For a number of years now they have had to negotiate and navigate these new forms of communication without any help from our formal education system. Young people have learnt the 'language' and the structural devices of the net. They have done this by themselves and with the help of their friends. Schools have been peculiarly absent in this whole process. The increasingly ubiquitous access to the internet has meant that a whole new resource filled with information exists pretty much within reach of all and without control. The possibilities are endless; the dangers fairly evident. And yet schools at large are denying the internet a place in the classroom and ignoring the real ways in which it is being used. Schools would rather not have anything to do with the internet, preferring to persist with paper and pen. This is just not going to work. It is also a remarkably poor way of moving forward. Making excuses about safety online and control will not do. Making excuses about the cost of improving school ICT facilities will not do. The world has moved on in the way in which it communicates,

---

1 Schools are dropping the ICT GCSE. See Jess Staufenberg, Computing Education in 'Steep Decline' after Reforms, Warns Report, *Schools Week* (8 May 2019). Available at: https://schoolsweek.co.uk/computing-education-in-steep-decline-following-government-reforms-warns-new-report/.

and digital proficiency is absolutely essential to anyone hoping to get on in that world. This is true not just for our young digital natives but also for those of us who are old enough to know a time before the internet – us digital migrants.

In all areas of our lives, we are moving towards digital communication and storage – and this is particularly true in the world of work. As a lecturer at Sheffield Hallam University, I now conduct the business of the course online. The course handbook is online, and all correspondence – including the submission of essays – is dealt with electronically. Meetings are conducted as paperless events with participants able to access an N-drive where the relevant materials are stored. All my records about the course are kept in my personal drive. Similar links enabling students to access the reading required for seminars and the PowerPoint slides for lectures are posted in advance, again in digital form. I am writing the manuscript which will become this book on a laptop. There is no way that I would handwrite my ideas and then type them up. This way I can shift lines around, cut and paste, delete and organise presentational features as I go. I am not telling you anything new here; my point is that this is now normal, it's standard procedure. Writing with a pen in school must seem to children like a very strange thing to do. It affords none of the abilities and capacities to rework and edit that I have just described. Young people no longer want to work that way because it does not make sense. It is slow and cumbersome. No wonder it is so difficult at times to get children to commit words to paper. The activity of using a pen is becoming increasingly isolated to the domain of schools. It is one more way in which schools are becoming distanced from the real world.

Technology is empowering us to take control in ways that were previously unimaginable. The problem that we have at the moment is that we are in a transitional period in which the rate of change is faster than most of us can comfortably keep up with. Those who remember a time before the internet are getting older. When the young watch people of their parents' and grandparents' generations fumble about with digital equipment and digital platforms, it is no wonder that they turn to their elders for help less and less. Older generations are, in part, being passed by and they are beginning to lose their authority to speak about the way the world is, or, rather, the young are becoming more critical about whether they are worth listening to.

Technology has already radically changed the way in which we live and the opportunities that we have. Nearly four and a half billion people are now connected to the internet, many of whom are accessing it through mobile technology on the move during their busy days.[2] Multifunctional devices such as smartphones and smartwatches combine the needs of the user. Our relationship to money and to shopping has already changed profoundly. You can successfully navigate your life for days without having any physical money about your person. Some places have stopped accepting cash altogether. We can regulate the heating and security functions in our homes. Shopping can be ordered and delivered without us stepping foot outside the house. You can preheat your car before you leave the house. Voice assistants answer our questions, digital maps help us find where we want to go, and mobile alerts help to keep the elderly safe. You can watch your CCTV remotely. The way we access entertainment and how we meet new people (including people to date) has all changed.

On the horizon we have the driverless car, the fully robotic factory and new realities that are both virtual and augmented. The change is unprecedented. The pace of change is unprecedented. Those most ready for this revolution are the young. They do not remember a time before the mobile phone and the internet. It is perfectly natural for them. Technology is their reality. They have grown up with it and it is part of the way in which they expect to communicate. It is the means by which we can keep in touch with the world at large, as surely we all agree. It's real and it's here to stay. Having said that, it

---

2   See https://www.statista.com/statistics/617136/digital-population-worldwide/.

will adapt, changing over and over again during our lifetimes.

There are a number of driving forces that are contributing to this current momentum.

Big data

Big data is the collection of vast swathes of information that indicate patterns of behaviour, gathered from our internet usage, that can be used to predict habits and identify trends. There are all sorts of potential uses for this – from providing businesses with vital information about their performance to rigging elections. Our young need to be alert to the potential uses and dangers of big data, and the ways in which data is and can be manipulated to their advantage or disadvantage. As part of the school curriculum we need to consider the general topic of communication. I guess this could be a mix of English, ICT, maths, business studies and science. However we locate it in the curriculum, we need to highlight how big data impacts on our daily lives and how it can be approached.

Artificial intelligence

It seems clear that artificial intelligence is going to usher in automation of simple measurable tasks and that 'intelligent' robots will soon be running and developing large-scale systems and tasks which were previously conducted by people. Developments such as self-driving cars, brain enhancements and genetic editing offer new solutions to global challenges, and new opportunities for people. On the flip side, there will undoubtedly be technologically generated unemployment and a downward pressure on income security and social agency. Can we establish links with local and national business so that schools can receive up-to-date information about jobs that are being generated by new technologies and also about those jobs that are being replaced?

Blockchain

Blockchain technology enables a system of 'safe', secure and visible links that support the transfer of information. It will rely on the creation of trust in making transactions in this new way. Blockchain will revolutionise a number of well-established areas of society. Some of the early applications include online voting systems, money transfers and automatic compensation for late and cancelled trains. Blockchain technology is going to have a huge impact on the workings of banking, insurance, real estate, health, energy and transport. Does your school staff know enough about the ways in which jobs are coming and going on the back of this? I'd imagine not in most cases. STEM (science, technology, engineering and maths) subjects are going to need to orientate themselves towards this developing change.

Virtual and augmented reality

Virtual reality (VR) is 3D and immersive. It has huge implications for enlivening school in an age that is characterised by a preference for more visual ways of accessing information. Most young people would much rather reach for sound and images over written text. VR is now being used in the training of medics and pilots, and in the aeronautics, rail maintenance, petrochemical and nuclear industries – usually using a VR headset. Augmented reality (AR) enhances real-world objects by adding a computer-generated element, such as images, animated graphics or sounds. Mixed reality is a combination of VR and AR.

Think of the potential applications of these developing technologies for your subject: to walk around a village during the plague, to be in the woods with Wordsworth, to see what the best pass choice in netball is from an actual position on the pitch, to watch over van Gogh's shoulder as he paints, to go down a mole's hole to see how they live ... The potential is endless and invigorating. In making things clear to see, these new technologies can make learning a fuller experience.

3D printing

The invention of 3D printing has opened up a number of potential applications. Computer-aided designs can be used to print out sophisticated shapes using a range of materials. This production model is being used successfully in a wide range of industries, including in sociocultural sectors, manufacturing and medicine, and also in the humanitarian and development sector to produce a range of medical items, prosthetics, spares and repairs.

One highly successful example of its application is the work of the LimbBo Foundation in Barnsley.[3] They work with Team Unlimbited to make functional prosthetic arms for children across the world. The 3D-printing technique means the cost of production is a fraction of what it would be to make such an intricate piece of machinery. Whilst the LimbBo Foundation is an inspirational change leader in making children's lives better, I think they provide an excellent example of how such technology can have everyday applications.

---

3   See https://www.limbbofoundation.co.uk/.

How should we respond to the changes brought by technology?

We are going to automate the work and we are going to humanise the jobs. This is the direction in which the world is moving, and education needs to become attuned to this momentum. There are three areas of human endeavour in which AI machines cannot compete, which will be most immediately significant in terms of humans retaining jobs. Firstly, there are those jobs and pursuits that demand creativity. This is much more than creative writing or painting. It would also cover new scientific discovery, for example. Things we don't know about and things that humans can take aesthetic pleasure from creating will stay within our parameters. Emotional intelligence is also distinctly ours. The ability to form social bonds is a key skill which machines cannot yet imitate. Also, those jobs that require physical dexterity will remain human pursuits. The rest will be automated.[4] As educators, we need to watch how the employment landscape develops so that we can offer a curriculum that feeds into the needs of society and allows our children the best chances of participating. We must make sure that we nurture our children's potential rather than set them up against AI machines. People will not be employed to do the work that a machine can do, so they need uniquely human skills.

The use of AI in the US education system is predicted to grow by up to 48% in the period 2018–2022.[5] Schools have begun to use AI machines to support pupils' learning. An individual visual AI helper can learn as it supports a child, developing a

---

4 Jamie Susskind, *Future Politics: Living Together in a World Transformed by Tech* (Oxford: Oxford University Press, 2018).
5 According to Technavio's Artificial Intelligence Market in the US Education Sector 2018–2022 report, quoted in Douglas Bonderud, Artificial Intelligence, Authentic Impact: How Educational AI Is Making the Grade, *Ed Tech* (12 August 2019). Available at: https://edtechmagazine.com/k12/article/2019/08/artificial-intelligence-authentic-impact-how-educational-ai-making-grade-perfcon.

stronger and stronger understanding of that learner. The AI robot can monitor learning, making it fit the individual, and it has the capacity to formulate ways forward when the pupil is struggling. It can also pass on all this information to the teacher, helping to inform their planning for progress with the class and shaping how they deliver the curriculum as a whole.

So how should we respond to this developing situation within the classroom? The 'sage on the stage' type of delivery – either by the teacher or via a live broadcast – could continue, but is this the best approach? In Californian schools, children spend up to a quarter of their time following individual learning programmes online.[6] These programmes move at an appropriate rate for the learner and with regard for their individual aptitudes and weaknesses. The data collected by these programmes can inform the work of the teachers. This is a step in the direction of collecting and collating a child's educational experience online. It also begins a move towards the teacher as a guide and away from their role as the expert who simply hands on information.

Edmodo (which is like Facebook for schools) has around 48 million users and includes media platforms for sharing materials and supporting students in interacting with learners outside of the classroom. Moodle has 65 million users; Brightspace has a further 15 million users.[7] This collaborative means of learning seems vastly preferred by the young. In their leisure time, many are gaming with others online, developing the narrative and enjoying the experience together. It is a familiar forum and one that feels comfortable.

In the future, humans will not have jobs that can be measured or that are based on rules – those will all have been automated. Schools need to be aware of the lifespan of jobs when

6   Maya Escueta, Vincent Quan, Andre Joshua Nickow and Philip Oreopoulos, *Education Technology: An Evidence-Based Review*, NBER Working Paper No. 23744 (August 2017). Available at: https://www.povertyactionlab.org/sites/default/files/publications/NBER-23744-EdTech-Review.pdf.
7   Richard Susskind and Daniel Susskind, *The Future of the Professions: How Technology Will Transform the Work of Human Experts* (Oxford: Oxford University Press, 2015), p. 7.

they are preparing young people for the adult world of work. The 'middleman' is under real pressure.

An education system designed for an industrial economy that is now being automated requires transformation, from a system based on facts and procedures to one that actively applies that knowledge to collaborative problem-solving.[8]

'Looking back at old-fashioned textbooks and the way that school would be measuring everyone all the time, teachers never really got to tell you what they thought or let you really have a go at things ...'

This just won't work as a model going forward – and our education system has to work. Therefore, the system must change to respond to the fact that the world is digital. Everything has moved online. It is where communication takes place.

'My work is now pretty much all online. That is where I find my work and where people find me. I need to get my social media and my website right. There is some work through word of mouth but even then, people look at the website.'

Young people understand the value of having a well-curated website and social media platforms. Their website will tell

8   Graham Brown-Martin, Education and the Fourth Industrial Revolution, Learning {Re}imagined (14 January 2018). Available at: https://medium.com/learning-re-imagined/education-and-the-fourth-industrial-revolution-cd6bcd7256a3.

you whether they are up to the job or not. It will communicate their values, demonstrate the work they are doing and indicate whether what they do is worth the price they are charging. They also need to be able to manicure their social media pages: to understand how Twitter reactions can be multiplied as well as when and how to release new material on their Facebook and Instagram pages. What time of day should they release new announcements if they want to have maximum impact in the United States as well as in Europe? Can they read and interpret their Twitter analytics and are they able to work with that data to improve clicks and time spent on their channels?

My interviewees know about algorithms and they understand the ways in which they work. They are thinking about how they are going to make that work for them. Many have a YouTube channel and, again, they are looking into ways of increasing views. They are making short films about their work because, in this increasingly visual world, people want to see what they are getting. Recently, I worked with a spoken word artist to make a short video for a presentation. The video lasted three minutes. It took us about five minutes to film it and then he spent another thirty minutes editing it together. We had our 'professional' looking video ready in well under an hour. That task would fit into an English lesson very easily. For that matter, creating a short film in under an hour would be a useful task in any subject area.

Young people are developing their understanding of their 'professional face' and that doesn't mean being completely corporate. It means that they are creating an identity that shows who they are and what they have to offer. Trust is at a premium online. Young people are trying to be open and honest about what they do and who they are.

'Whatever you are selling, your competitors are selling the same thing. The way you stand out is you sell yourself. The customer is looking for someone they can trust to deliver the best product or service … really, they are buying into you … you have to look good … get it right.'

My interviewees were learning to design webpages and make films for themselves, although some have been working with film editors to arrange sound and work out the shot transitions. They are learning those skills as they go and soon they will be able to do that for themselves as well. They have access to the software package. But schools should be playing a role here. There is no level playing field and many of our economically disadvantaged pupils are not going to have the access to equipment and support outside of school settings. Even if it were just in an attempt to right this inequality, I think that schools should offer support in developing the capacity to create digital forums such as websites and social media platforms, alongside learning about the ways in which a person can connect with others safely across the net.

Most of our young people, however, do now have excellent access to digital opportunities. This was certainly the case with my interviewees, pretty much regardless of their family's economic situation. Digital access has become a necessity. Those young people who do have it spend a lot of time working on digital platforms – too much, really.[9] They can be addictive in terms of checking them, adapting content, adding new posts and fretting over the number of views and amount of engagement that they are getting. They have had to learn all of this for themselves, with no help from school. They told me that they supposed their teachers thought that

---

9   Of course, you can now look at the analytics of your smartphone usage. By 11.46 a.m. on the day I'm writing this, I have spent forty-four minutes making phone calls, eighteen minutes on WhatsApp, eight minutes on Instagram, five minutes on Facebook, and so on. I can now monitor my screen time and see whether I am spending too much time on my phone.

they can just 'do' the internet because they are of the digital native generation – they were born into the digital world. It seemed to them like their teachers just assumed that the pupils would have a better understanding of technology than they did themselves.

Despite the general presumption that young people can just 'do it', our children often struggle to make effective use of the internet. This belief is particularly erroneous and dangerous given the digital imperative. Pupils need to be able to do research online and have a critical eye. Schools need to be involved in helping them learn how to do this, and they need to do more than issue a vague warning about the internet being dangerous. Schools need to look into explicitly training pupils in how to be alert and safe online. This, I think, needs to be a distinct aspect of the curriculum, and the learning that happens within it needs to be planned into the work of other subjects.

I spent some time in the interviews reflecting on the use of personal electronic devices in lessons. Schools have been somewhat slow to accept the educational uses that smartphones can have, seeing them as primarily a tool for entertainment or distraction.

Here are the results of my question about phone use:

- At school they wouldn't let you have your phone at all (45%).
- At school they let you have your phone, but you couldn't use it in lessons (45%).
- At school we could use phones in lessons to look something up when the teacher said we could (8%).
- At school we were allowed to use our phones in lessons when we needed to (2%).

'School was always funny about phones too. I think it was because phones were for fun and private use before schools thought about using them for education. I think that this reflects the way schools treat the internet. On the whole, I only got to use the computers to do research; to replace the library, if you like.'

I think that we have all become four-dimensional. That fourth dimension is the imprint that we leave of ourselves everywhere: Twitter, Instagram, Facebook, a personal website, Reddit, emails, etc. Being away from all of that must feel very unnatural when it is an extension of who you are. To be apart from this fourth dimension is to feel cut off.

'Not having your phone is really hard. I have been brought up with it. My phone is part of me, really. If I run out of battery or leave it at home, it is really annoying.'

It doesn't make a great deal of sense to be prevented from having your phone at your disposal. Information is so freely available these days. If I need to know something, then I just look it up that minute. I can collect data from random and various sources. I think that schools need to teach children about the utility of the internet, and not just tell them to be wary of 'bad people' and cons. They need to know how to research, how to manipulate information to their advantage, how to make websites and how to gain as much positive attention for their work as possible. We need a proactive and engaged approach to teaching about the possibilities (some would say necessities) of the internet and digital literacy.

It schools want to remain relevant, the single biggest pressure point has to be their use of the internet and digital communication. This is the means through which the world actually communicates. Laptops and mobile phones have long since replaced paper and pen. They have also broadened, immeasurably, the ways in which we can interact with others and present ourselves. Young people spend much more time learning and communicating through digital means in their lives outside school than they do in it. Ignoring these developing approaches to learning means that schools are falling far short of their aim to help their pupils become articulate. To be articulate these days is to be proficient online.

We also find ourselves in an interesting time: we are still in a transitional period, in which the older generation is having to adapt to new forms of communication whilst the young have grown up with online interactions and regard them as natural. There is fast coming a time when no one will remember the pre-internet age. It will have become a natural part of life. The internet has radically changed how we communicate and how we find and access knowledge. It is putting a distance between what is seen as relevant today and more traditional curricular content.

'I enjoyed reading *Silas Marner* in English and writing a newspaper report about Eppie going missing, but what I really needed was to know about how GitHub works ... if I had known that earlier it would have saved me so much time with collaborative work ... with being better informed about everything ... about who is out there. Some thought needs to be put into how the adult world really communicates. Who reads a newspaper anyway?'

The young people who I interviewed were largely in agreement that remembering facts seemed to be the purpose of school; that and passing exams. In truth I don't think either of those things will turn out to be that useful anymore. Remembering stuff is not an essential skill. You can just look it up, check it over and then have information presented to you and for others in any number of ways. Young people say that their exam results haven't actually been seen by many people since they left school. They are more likely to have to demonstrate what they have achieved since they left school. Employers and clients also seem to be more interested in evidence of their online proficiency than in their exam results. Where qualifications are required in certain professions – such as accountancy, teaching or medicine – my interviewees still appreciated the limit of the value of the qualification itself, seeing it as no more than a gateway.

Cathy, a wedding designer, told me about how she developed her business online. Having left college she taught herself to sew and began to make cushions to sell online. This led to a Swiss company seeing her work and ordering cushions for the chairs that they made. Soon Cathy's small flat was full of cushions.

Once Cathy began her wedding design business, she was picking up just about all her work online. She tried for two years to make her website and social media channels as corporate and impressive as she could. This was what English lessons had told her was important in making a good impression. At GCSE it is called writing to persuade. Her company just about broke even. As she relaxed into the job, she began to make her content more personal. On Instagram, she would talk directly to camera about her daily life and the bookings coming in. You would see her making the bunting for weddings or setting up the table and chair arrangements. Her business began to pick up. What she was learning was that people buy into the personal. They buy into what they can see. Her business really started to bloom. We are communicating through a medium that is both visual but *also*, at times, highly manipulative. If potential customers can see both what is being offered and the people behind it, it's likely to influence their buying decisions. Cathy was learning this and learning to adapt the ways in which she presented herself.

'I have had to develop a critical eye. The internet isn't always honest, and you have to be able to sniff out where the dishonesty is. Everyone is showing you their best self. It is fast and emotional. You have to be able to see past the algorithms that are haunting you.'

Our young people report that they could have done with a lot more support in school regarding looking at how the internet really works.

'There should have been a lesson or a subject that is all about organising your online life ... it's a life skill these days.'

Our young entrepreneurs have needed to know all kinds of things about the internet. They have had to learn that you don't have long to make an impact with an audience. Attention is short. People want to find what they are looking for and move on quickly. How do you cater for that? How do you hook people in? The internet also has broadened, and sometimes contradicted, what they were taught about audience and context in English lessons. Audiences can be vast if you get your message right. Your stuff can pass before the eyes of so many people, without them having directly gone looking for it. How does this impact on how you should present yourself? People are searching through random pages and links. Their movement around the internet is in some ways much more focused on topics, and the range of sources is ever expanding. There is, however, the potential to veer off down sidetracks. The act of reading now involves a different set of manoeuvres.

'To tell you the truth, I don't think that my English teacher knew anything about this ...'

We are faced with a whole new reading context. The internet is a more interactive environment for readers and writers; there is a genuine blurring of the distinction between the two, caused by the capacity in online spaces for people to comment and join in. Our concept of reader and writer needs to be much broader than that which is currently taught in school. We also have to get rid of the idea of the generic reader. Whilst we want to get as many people as possible to see our online content, our young entrepreneurs have to find target audiences and niche markets to talk to, then try to develop the size of those audiences. This is not what is presented in school. The audiences spoken of in school tend to be static: fixed and quantifiable.

'In school we tended to find information on the internet. We should also look at the validity of the "information" that we discover.'

There seems to me to be a remarkable lack of funding for ICT services in schools. We know that writing in exercise books is second best. We need to go past worrying about the question of how to keep children safe whilst online. Online safety is important, of course, but we also have to develop the skills to understand why we are there and how to get the most from this remarkable game-changing resource.

Young people know that in most instances they are far ahead of most of their teachers when it comes to digital competence. Schools need to invest in having expert teachers in this area. They also need to invest in making sure that all teachers understand the digital imperative and that all teachers learn, unlearn and relearn what the digital environment can offer them in their classrooms.

'School's like the olden days. We're always writing everything down in little books with a pen [laughs]...'

Mary

Mary is ten and she is from Huddersfield. She knows. She wasn't one of my interviewees, but I met her in a primary school and just had to include her words as she's so right. Writing things down with paper and pen is no longer how we communicate. If you are to contribute to, and participate in, the world around you, there are now different tools and methods with which to make your voice heard. Paper and pen has become a wasteful and increasingly peculiar choice. The very permanence of paper, once its strong point, has become a weakness. It is neither quick enough nor adaptable enough to suit the ways in which we anticipate that we can communicate. It costs too much money and is slow and cumbersome.

'Well, no – I hardly write anything with a pen. You wouldn't, would you? Certainly not anything important – not for business – maybe a note to say I've gone out but not really then either – you'd just text, wouldn't you? I even text my mum when I'm upstairs and I want her to make me a cup of tea.'

The post-truth world has thrown up the idea that if you want to be believed then people need to see and hear the words coming out of your mouth rather than in a written text. A good example of this would be the much-anticipated investigation, led by Robert Mueller, into Russian interference in the US election of 2016. The final report was well over 400 pages long and it would appear that very few people actually read it. Instead, the majority of the electorate watched Attorney General William Barr's summary announcement.[10] Whilst Barr's speech mischaracterised what was in the report, this was the extent of most people's exposure to it. Once Mueller was subpoenaed and had to testify in front of Congress, the Democrats were mostly pleased because the American public would finally get to see and hear what Mueller had to say.

There are two things to note here. Firstly, it is clear that whilst most people wanted to know about the extent of Donald Trump's involvement in this matter, they were not prepared to read about it at length. They wanted a summary. Such is the way in which news is consumed these days. Secondly, there is genuine value in the American public seeing and hearing Mueller testify. The public will judge the situation based on what he has to say and how convincing he is before Congress. The truth and the facts are becoming less relevant than the appearance of things. This exemplifies the way in which effective communication is made. You need to know how audiences will react and how much they will interact. One might suspect that Trump, in concealing some truths, relied upon the audience's general lack of full attention.

The digital and tech giants are becoming some of the biggest companies in the world. Only 16 countries have a GDP that is worth more than Apple's market value.[11] Increasingly, these global enterprises are seen as malevolent monopolies

---

10 See Katie Reilly, Read Attorney General William Barr's Full Remarks Ahead of the Mueller Report Release, *Time* (18 April 2019). Available at: https://time.com/5573085/attorney-general-william-barr-transcript-mueller-report/.

11 Erica Alini, Apple Hits $1 Trillion in Value. Only 16 Countries Are Worth More, *Global News* (2 August 2018). Available at: https://globalnews.ca/news/4367056/apple-1-trillion-market-cap/.

– with massive profits that go untaxed – which manipulate our behaviours for their own benefit. Big data and algorithms track our interests and record our digital movements. Whilst some might fear this, our young people consider the digital environment to be inescapable; entwined with their vision of their potential and their futures. Our young want to learn to work with digital systems.

If, as Sugata Mitra's research would suggest, children are capable of learning how to surf the web by themselves (more on which in Chapter 3), then we need to think about what teachers need to add to this gathering of information, and develop ways of embedding this into practice.[12]

'I did most of my best work at home, thinking about what we'd done in class.'

The young are alert to the fact that they need to make a quick impression in their online dealings. Those who are able to create websites and a presence on social media – and then manipulate their use of those forums – are at a strong advantage. This is what 'writing' is going to be in the coming years. Can we help young people to be literate on the internet? This means so much more than teaching them about correct spelling and punctuation, or offering generic lessons about writing to persuade.

This is the central issue facing schools today. If school is going to be worth the young's while, we have to make full and central use of ICT. It is how we communicate in the real world, so it is essential that children develop a sense of their own capacity to manipulate digital forums to their advantage. If we continue to ignore the internet, then school will become entirely redundant; a failed utilitarian project. It won't be worth talking about the other things that school might be for,

12 Sugata Mitra, The Future of Schooling: Children and Learning at the Edge of Chaos, *Prospects*, 44(4) (2014): 547–558.

such as cultivating a love of learning, or encouraging personal growth beyond jobs or an appreciation of beauty. Remove the internet from the classroom and it becomes too far removed from reality.

Future school I

This morning, our team is meeting in town at the library resource centre. It is my turn to be the team leader and I have booked a meeting room from 9 a.m. until 10 a.m. The team is made up of children from my local area. We no longer have a physical school, but I meet many more peers than I would have done sat in a classroom. Today's team have opted into this project on the environment, which is one of the core strands of the curriculum. We only have the meeting room for an hour, so I need to get prepared in advance in order to get everyone out and about quickly.

We are working on a project that will be recorded in our individual portfolios. We will all leave school with an online portfolio that documents the projects and initiatives that we have been involved in (exams have long since been abolished). Our teacher notes the amount of time we have invested in different aspects of our education and the level of competence we have developed. They look at things like self-determination and confidence alongside the 'learning' that we do. The portfolio also features examples of the work that we have produced, including evidence recorded as text, image and sound. When we are looking for work, the online portfolio can easily be edited and adapted to demonstrate the potentially useful experiences and expertise that we have.

During my meetings with my mentor, it was noted – and added to my portfolio – that I have a growing interest in business and environmental issues. The portfolio software is mindful of this when thinking about allocating the experiences that I will have at school. Whilst the programme is developing my foundational knowledge of word and number, it is also building my expertise in the areas of most interest to me, and in which I am proving most adept.

As physical writing has become redundant, there is no longer a problem with standard spelling or presentation. Artificial intelligence has made this an obsolete consideration. My 'written texts' are spoken to the online portfolio and the grammatical and presentational features are arranged for me. The technology makes suggestions about sentences and ideas in my text, with which I either agree or disagree. I talk to the portfolio about the positioning of text and images and it moves these around at my direction. I also work with the portfolio to make a multimedia presentation to introduce today's project to my new colleagues.

One of the strands that we are developing is concern for our local environment. We are thinking about our town and, in particular with this project, the natural world in our environment. This morning the team are assembled for a briefing. We are researching the reasons why bees are disappearing from our locality. We want to find out reasons why this might be happening, and we want to promote ways in which we can support the growth of the bee population locally. This idea came from one of the team members and was agreed upon by us all as a worthy project.

Chapter 3
CONNECTIONS

How do our young people learn to be sociable? How do they learn to present themselves? How do they think of things to say when meeting new people? How does being sociable impact upon our well-being and confidence?

Young people want to make a connection. Young people want to make connections. Young people want to contribute. They want to be included. They want to look after each other. They want a chance to join in and be a part of the world. This is how they perceive the idea of making something of themselves. Interviewee after interviewee told me about the developing network that they had established or joined, which kept them going in terms of spirit and often in terms of fresh opportunities. In a world of self-employment, which can be isolating, it becomes crucial that you seek out others.

A couple of things particularly stood out under the theme of making connections. Firstly, it is clearly important that you can build a supportive network as you are getting going in work. If you are going to thrive, or even just get started, you will need people around you who are willing to help, support you and promote what you are doing. You will need guidance. Secondly, the sense of a 'business community' is strong in the young. The idea of sharing with other developing businesses, even when that means making a little less money, was clearly a route that the young are keen to tread. Maybe they feel that they have strength in numbers as they take on an adult world that has become largely closed to them?

School should be the perfect place to help children learn to collaborate. Pupils need to work together and understand that within a project, and within their work lives, different people will have different roles and responsibilities. Being open to that idea builds your capacity to think about what role you will take on. Being connected opens your eyes to the ways in which you can lean on other people's knowledge and expertise whilst developing your own. After all, we can all brush our teeth, but most of us can't make toothpaste!

'Putting yourself out there is the thing ... if your hand is up often enough, I reckon you can soon become the 'go-to' guy. People start to understand that you are committed ... it's about being seen to be involved.'

My interviewees told me that their schools shied away from collaborative work most of the time because of the difficulty of not having everyone passively sitting in seats and focusing on their individual progress.[1] It seems that 'top sets' particularly suffered: teachers felt that they didn't need to do group work as the pupils were compliant enough to sit through passive lessons. Group work was often used for reflection; pupils simply gathered round to critique each other's work. Rarely was group work an integral part of the set-up or way of working on a topic. Where there was group work, often everyone in the group was just doing the same thing. Is there scope in your lessons for collaborative work in which pupils have different roles to fulfil?

1   See Grainne Hallahan, Why It's Time to Say Goodbye to Group Work, TES (10 March 2018). Available at: https://www.tes.com/news/why-its-time-say-goodbye-group-work. This article sums up the sorts of negative responses that some teachers and schools have towards group work. The concern expressed is about an inability to make it work, rather than doubt over its inherent value. Being expected to work as part of a group is an essential skill for the workplace. Young people are learning collaboratively both locally and across global networks and online platforms.

'Some of the practical hands-on techniques and skills I began learning in school. I was taught the basics in a number of arts-based subjects. These have been the most explicit of the skills that I learnt that I have since been able to develop and put into practice. But I have had to build a network of connections around me for all sorts of reasons. There are, obviously, all kinds of very specific skills that I have needed that were nowhere near touched upon at school. I guess you leave school with a raw talent that needs to be refined and honed, hopefully towards expertise.'

Sometimes you just need advice and help when you don't have the knowledge and skills required. But are there opportunities to approach parts of your curriculum in which the answer is not known, or there is no agreed upon answer, or the question is devised by the pupils? Where can we build in investigative learning? If we do, then pupils can work together to develop their thinking and their skills. And, whilst the pupils are approaching work in this way, can we be explicit about the way in which they are working? Can you coach them in teamwork? Can we point the pupils to the real-world applications of collaborative working?

'I get much of the technical information and skills that I need from the internet. Often there are YouTube videos that come in handy.'

'You can grow your own understanding and expertise by solving problems as they arise. I do think that there is merit in just getting on with it. Sometimes I've taken on a job and I didn't really have any idea whether I was going to be able to do the work. You just have to back yourself sometimes.

If you can see the potential of getting skilled up quickly, then you can do that. Otherwise, you need to rustle up some help or get one of your contacts to show you, or even do the work for you. Between us we'll get it done. That always strikes me as a better bet than turning down commissions that will just go elsewhere. I think if you turn down work, the client is far less likely to come back another time.'

Can we support access to networks in sectors that pupils are interested in? Let's take the example of an open-ended project to do some charity work in the local community. Pupils take responsibility for finding charities with which they would like to work. They create a shortlist and make decisions about which one they will help. They could be encouraged to draw up a list of people who they need to contact – anyone who would be useful to talk to or might help them make progress. Then they divide up the work of making these contacts and report back on their discussions and correspondence. Depending on the nature of the charity, this project could fit into different curricular areas. For example, if the pupils choose a charity which helps children with disabilities to participate in sport, then this might well be the subject of a PE lesson as much as it might fit within English, humanities or general studies. The connections that are generated by the pupils will demonstrate how to work through a process to develop networks of people, as well as how to identify leads using the internet.

'It is sometimes hard to find your niche market, past it being on the internet somewhere. Likewise, you can often struggle to find those who are operating in the same field and are prepared to team up and collaborate. The internet has given us all access to so much, but I also think in some ways it has isolated us all as well.'

Over and over, the young people I spoke to told me about the wonderful people they have met through networking who proved to be useful to them. Listening to their responses, it struck me that these 'wonderful people' were either clearly in it to make money from this connection or were genuinely acting as an advocate and trying to give the young person a helping hand. An advocate is a healthy role model. Surely, we are well placed to fulfil this role in school?

Another benefit of networking is that you can't know everything that is going on in your field. Advances are being made all the time. Changing industry norms and technological advances can mean that you are quickly out of date. Young people have the perception that they can just start up, regardless of prior experience. I met a number of successful people who have no formal training in the work that they are doing, or any relevant qualifications. They have learnt from the internet and by connecting with others who have shown them what to do. Then they are up and running. It strikes me that the sort of person who does this has a good deal of drive and is resourceful and responsive. But it does require you to be connected.

'Things are changing fast and I am sure that I will have to adapt. There does seem to be a tendency for anyone to think that they can do anything these days. With the YouTube videos that I mentioned earlier, it is possible to pick up the basics in all sorts of areas. That means people are less likely to pay for expertise if they feel that they can do something for themselves. If my skills were no longer needed, then I understand that I might need to reinvent myself.'

And the young will listen mainly to their peers. Being 'expert' for them is being able to actively demonstrate what you do. The proof is in the pudding.

'I am going to say that it depends on what it is that I need help with. In general, I'd say that I'd ask my peers and I'd search online before I'd ask anyone from my parents' generation. It might just be that they can't use the internet and their phones properly half the time or it might be because things have changed so much, even in the short time I have been involved.'

But access to a network is never handed to you. You need to go out and look for it. Connectedness is waiting out there, but you have to go to it. In school, can we explore how to make connections and how to grow a network? Can that be built into the curriculum and, again, can we be explicit in talking about how important it is to have the ability to make connections with people?

'I started a networking meeting. There are about 250 people in the group ... photographers, florists, musicians, hospitality ... about 40 attend each time. It connects me with all the people I need to collaborate with.'

'I insist that the hotels that I work with do not use things like plastic straws. That seems to be fine; you just have to say that's what you want. I just think that people don't always think about it.'

A number of the interviewees could name people who had influenced them, and they were reflective about the nature of their impact. These are the advocates that I mentioned earlier. They not only had an influence on the young person and their ideas, but they then helped to promote them. In these days when the adult world can seem so loath to give the young a chance, it is important that there are advocates out there. Everyone needs a cheerleader, and an influential one at that.

The young are more than happy to collaborate rather than be in competition all the time. During a number of the interviews there were interruptions for networking conversations and promises of collaboration and meeting up soon. This is why the world of the start-up business has moved to the coffee shop. Schools need to design learning opportunities that allow our young people to achieve genuine outcomes by collaborating in real-world situations. This is key if we are to add to young people's ability to thrive. Relevance has to be made explicit.

The young are often living in atomised social isolation because of decreasing social mobility. They can become hampered by the sense that they can't grow up and become their own person because they have to live at home with their parents, with little hope of moving out. But this growing frustration is leading the young to turn away from the aspirations that society has laid out for them. The young are connecting with each other. They are networking and forging alliances, learning to grow their work and personal lives together. They speak to each other, listen to each other and trust each other. They bond over the shared experience of being young these days. Our successful young understand that finding a community and contributing to it is a healthy way forward.

In our schools, let's get the pupils to collaborate. They can be engaged in work that has a real purpose and a definite end point. It needs to be important; more important than a test! This might include such 'real' purposes as exhibitions, talks, publications or manufacturing products (both in the arts and in design technology/science and, indeed, across the curriculum). A genuine sense of purpose will always lift the quality of the work and the thinking that the children engage in. As I mention elsewhere, children do too much passive sitting in our classrooms. It is one of the ways in which schools do not meet the needs of the modern learner, or mirror the ways in which the modern learner actually learns.

In some places it is hard to network if you don't know where to start and you don't have practical routes into meeting people. A number of my interviewees noted that it had taken them a long time to find the people they needed. This was largely to do with not knowing how to go about finding those people or not believing that they were out there.

'In some places there just isn't a scene in the area that you are interested in developing. I'd say that you should just go out and make a scene: you start it up and see if there are others who are interested. That way, you'll be at the centre of things in your area. You're not going to find your crowd if you don't speak up and go looking for them.'

For my interviewees who were living in rural areas, this difficulty was seemingly heightened. Educational research suggests that the further away you live from urban centres, the more difficult it becomes to do well in exams.[2] This is fairly self-evident in poor countries in which it can be difficult to get any schooling at all, but it is also true of more affluent Western countries. Sugata Mitra suggests that an electronic education can help to solve the problem of accessing a good education regardless of where you are from by creating a community of learners.

Have a look at Sugata Mitra's pioneering work in India, in which he plotted test scores against the distance that children lived from New Delhi. Initially he put the regional disparity down to lower commitment and expertise in the teachers who were prepared to live in more rural areas. Well-trained teachers found it easiest to move wherever they wanted, so teacher training would not present an immediate solution whilst rural schools remained undesirable places to teach. But something else was going on.

Mitra found that children can teach themselves if they have access to the internet. With no knowledge of how to operate a computer, or of the potential that it has, children are able to quickly start making productive use of an internet connection to find things out for themselves. I think that it is important to conceptualise learning as something that we make, rather than something that we receive. This fits in with the vision of the School in the Cloud, which was formed off the back of Mitra's research.

The School in the Cloud proclaims, 'We're turning the world of education on its head through self-organised learning environments (SOLEs). Why not join our global experiment?'[3] It boasts a community of over 18,000 members who are sharing their projects across the globe. Children are asked to work together to come up with answers to 'big questions'. In

2 Mitra, The Future of Schooling.
3 See https://www.theschoolinthecloud.org/.

their various locations around the world, the children don't have to stay in their seats, they can look at each other's work and they can negotiate who does what in the learning process. I find this approach inspiring and it is surely much closer to the model of learning that they will have to make use of in the workplace. It teaches you about having a voice, about being a team player and about the need to design approaches to your own learning and thinking. Nobody is handing the 'knowledge' to you; you are expected to be far more active and collaborative in your learning.

> '**I am starting to pick up a fair bit of work – repeat work at that – through Crowdworker ... you know what that is?**'

I didn't, but I do now. It is an online agency that connects businesses with talented freelancers.[4] They are tapping into the increasingly prevalent idea that companies need to actively recruit and then try to retain freelancers. Connectedness is an essential aspect of modern living. Networking is important for giving a business a firm foundation from which to grow. Our children must learn to collaborate as they explore their own learning.

Some schools – such as those in the XP Schools Trust – are beginning to move their curriculum towards this project-based, collaborative form of learning. A child in Year 8 at XP School in Doncaster will follow five cross-curricular themes that are approached as expeditions and involve a good deal of time off-site, making visits to locations which are relevant to the work that they are doing. The expeditions have some genuine outcomes that go way past preparing the children for examinations. By the end of Year 8, you will end up having: delivered a speech; created a sculpture; written a short story; designed a site report; invented a trivia-based

4 See http://www.crowdworker.com.

board game; written an essay about conflict; and built and designed a robot. Much of this is in the national curriculum, but the approach of collaborating and finding things out for yourself is what makes this a refreshing approach to learning. It is an approach that those in the adult workplace are telling us that they would have benefitted from.

Future school II

This term I am working on the communication skills that I am likely to need as I decide whether to take up the government offer of the school-leaver start-up business loan, which I should qualify for given the strength of my portfolio. I have opted into a module aimed at developing my online presence and I also want support with checking the safety of my profiles.

Our session today is from the core foundational topic of 'communication'. We are learning the basics of presenting ourselves in person and online. We are in the education room of the local coffee shop, making use of their online connection hub. I have worked through the online module at home in advance and today we are going to look at the questions that I have, based on my reading.

The unit begins with a consideration of the potential reach of the usual mediums. I want some help to think about:

- How to access the local community effectively.
- Making contact with a more global clientele.
- Maximising how many views I'm getting via search engines.
- How to find the forums and communities that I think might be interested in joining my project.

We then move on to look at ways of getting help in extending our reach, including the potential support that can be offered by AI services in developing my profiles across the different platforms. I also want to know about the potential reach of promoted tweets – where does the traffic lie? Will it really be worth the cost at outset?

Safety and authenticity are concerns and we cover questions such as:

- How can you trust that a person is telling the truth?
- How can you spot when a 'person' is actually a bot?

After the tuition session, I add all this information to the growing directory of online links in my portfolio, and my tutor comments and adds to my credit score. I then write a brief plan about the next steps in my project and how I am going to make use of what I have just learnt.

Chapter 4

MONEY MANAGEMENT

In my opinion, the United States and many Western nations have a financial disaster coming, caused by our educational system's failure to adequately provide a realistic financial education program for students.

Robert T. Kiyosaki[1]

Now that is a prophetic remark, considering that it was made in 2001. Why do we continue to let our children leave school without any formal support around money management? Wealth is increasingly held by fewer and fewer people. Access to wealth can be a real problem for the young. The main form of access they seem to have is to credit, and thus to all-consuming debt.

The Money Advice Trust issued a report in 2016 in which it revealed that 18- to 24-year-olds are building up significant debts at a relatively early age and, as a consequence, they are beginning to suffer significant financial concerns, even though most are actively trying to manage their spending.[2] The survey involved over 2,000 young people and indicated that their average debt was £2,969. This figure did not include any student loans or mortgages. The survey showed that 37% of those surveyed were already in a substantial amount of debt. The worry over the debt had caused significant loss of sleep and energy. However, another cause for

---

1   Robert T. Kiyosaki, *The Business School for People Who Like Helping People* (Scottsdale, AZ: Cashflow Technologies Inc, 2001).
2   National Debtline and Money Advice Trust, *Borrowed Years: A Spotlight Briefing on Young People, Credit and Debt* (August 2016). Available at: http://www.moneyadvicetrust.org/SiteCollectionDocuments/Research%20 and%20reports/Borrowed%20Years%2c%20Young%20people%20credit%20 and%20debt%2c%20Aug%202016.pdf.

concern was that too few of the young people surveyed were seeking help or talking about their debts.

> 'There's no chance of getting a house. And a mortgage ... it's not even a consideration. Any money I might have needs to be there for reinvesting in the business. I certainly can't raise a deposit.'

If there is no chance of buying a house or saving money, then what is it that young people are actually working for? Most of my interviewees painted a picture of a fairly hand-to-mouth existence when describing their finances.

Austerity has squeezed us all, but it has been a particular problem for our young people. They are more likely to be in a low-paid job than their older counterparts.[3] They are also legally discriminated against by the fact that the minimum wage is lower for those under the age of 24. Car insurance for young and inexperienced drivers makes owning a car a genuinely unaffordable expense for some. University students are paying record-high tuition fees and are scrabbling about in part-time jobs – sometimes two or three of them, on top of their studies – for enough money on which to subsist. This must have a detrimental impact on their ability to study with any strength or focus.

The offer of financial support from the big banks and traditional credit institutions is harder to come by these days, especially if you are young. Lloyds Bank tripled the interest rate on their overdrafts in November 2017. In December 2019 HSBC followed suit, quadrupling overdraft interest rates for

---

3 Georgia Gould, *Wasted: How Misunderstanding Young Britain Threatens Our Future* (London: Abacus, 2016).

some customers.[4] One radio advertisement for Lloyds bank features a conversation between two young people mulling over whether their parents would be able to help them get on the property ladder.[5] So-called springboard or family mortgages seem to be increasingly common. The banks, it would seem, recognise that they are going to have to squeeze money out of the last generation because the young don't have any. They certainly don't have enough to spend on a mortgage – at least not without some help from the Bank of Mum and Dad – and have largely given up on the idea. All of this could be seen as a form of social control.

When you look at the collective practices of the young in their work lives, it becomes clear that the growth in the number of self-employed workers has not happened by chance. The young feel pushed out by society at large but they also view working for themselves as a positive choice.

'There are plenty of times when I might not get paid for some of the work that I do. There's also a lot of "mates' rates" going on with the people that I collaborate with. You have to work out if it's going to be worth doing a loss-leader if there is going to be more work coming from it. Conferences might let you have a stand in exchange for a demonstration or some other product. Paying for support with your website, advertising and even making a YouTube video will cost money that you can't directly redeem. But it might mean that you get

4   For some trends in interest rate changes, see: Ben Chapman, HSBC to Introduce 40% Overdraft Interest Rate, Quadrupling Costs for Some Customers, *The Independent* (5 December 2019). Available at: https://www. independent.co.uk/news/business/news/hsbc-overdraft-fees-interest-rate-rise-charges-christmas-spending-a9233821.html.
5   See Patrick Collinson, Lloyds Unveils 100% Mortgage for First-Time Buyers, *The Guardian* (28 January 2019). Available at: https://www.theguardian.com/money/2019/jan/28/lloyds-unveils-100-mortgage-for-first-time-buyers.

loads of work off the back of it. It's about thinking it through and learning from what works and what turns out not to work ... all a bit of a risk though.'

The boom in self-start-up as a prospect and a potential way out of the financial gloom becomes increasingly attractive. It might well be that austerity has taught our young the value of 'having enough', as I detected this as a growing concept. They are far from greedy. Indeed, the troubling aspect is that it sounded to me as if they were talking about simply having enough to get by on: to keep paying the bills and keep their enterprise going. But on the positive side, our young are interested in working at micro-levels, specialising in niche markets. There is a real growth in start-up companies working in units next to each other and supporting each other's initiatives. In Nottingham, Sneinton Market is flourishing with all sorts of businesses, run by the young and by families working together.[6] The sense of community that thrives there encourages a 'scene', and the bustle is growing, benefiting them all.

On the topic of personal finances, we need to acknowledge that there is no level playing field in this area either. Being well-off these days is hard to attain, and it's not necessarily contingent on talent or hard work. We also need to be explicit with our pupils: for the overwhelming majority of them, this is going to be the case and they are going to have to be prepared it and for the fact that they need to actively engage with the world of work, whether they are looking for paid employment or want to make a go of things by themselves. Whilst more and more of our pupils will be freelancing in the future, they need to understand that opportunities are not equally stacked. They are going to have to grind out a career. That is a hard message to have to discuss but it is a much truer one than the old story of work hard in school and you'll get a good job.

6   See https://sneintonmarket.com/.

'We didn't have any money to start with, so it's taking a little longer to build things up … the bank was never quite sure that we could match our ambition.'

I think that it falls to schools to talk explicitly about money management.[7] Schools must provide a clear guide as to how to look after personal finances. Young people need to understand the value of money if they are not to spend the rest of their lives in debt that cannot be shifted. This is particularly crucial at the present moment. The pending disappearance of money[8] and the introduction of bitcoin will have implications for the ways in which we teach about value. So how will we teach value when we don't have a physical currency? I am sure that there is a perfectly good set of answers to this question. But it seems that, at the moment, we just aren't talking about it.

'I have eight bank accounts for different things … I know that sounds mad, but it feels secure. I know what I have for the different areas of my life.'

Our children will need to know how Blockchain works. They will also need an appreciation of how to choose a mortgage that they can afford or, more realistically, how much rent they can manage to pay. Fewer and fewer young people are bothering to get a pension. They see the constant threat of the

---

7   Whilst finance management has been a part of the national curriculum since 2014 – as discussed in Owen Burek, 15 Vital Money Lessons You Should Have Been Taught in School, *Save the Student* (10 October 2019). Available at: https://www.savethestudent.org/money/15-money-lessons.html – none of my interviewees recognised that they had had any support around their financial well-being.

8   Kevin Mercadante, The Future of Cash – Will It Disappear or Become Obsolete?, *Money Under 30* (22 May 2019). Available at: https://www.moneyunder30.com/what-is-the-future-of-cash.

state pension age going up and do not trust that any schemes are going to offer any real value by the time it comes to claiming them. Fewer and fewer young people are getting insurance of any kind, past the mandatory ones such as car insurance. Even then, not being able to pay for the insurance will limit access to vehicle ownership. Driving is important for freedom of movement and for a business to be mobile.

More and more of our young people are self-employed, which means that they will need to know about the annual cycle of paying tax. They need to know how to put money aside for paying their tax bill. They need to know how to set up a business for tax purposes. They also need to know what they can claim as tax-exempt expenses. None of this information is offered at school.

> 'I am lucky to have had a good start with help from my parents – the Bank of Mum and Dad I think it's called, at least that's what my dad said – but it did mean that it took me a fair while to understand about accounting.'

Given the needs we've outlined here, how do you manage to keep your head above water? How do you invest time and money in order to achieve more further down the line? These are questions that schools should address as we face huge uncertainty about the financial well-being of the UK and, indeed, the world.

For most young people the idea of long-term financial planning has been reduced to the month ahead. Where is the rent coming from? How stable is my job/business? What is my plan B for when things go wrong? How many days are there until I get paid? Will the client pay on time? If they don't, what am I going to do? This is subsistence management and it is stressful as a norm. It has a detrimental impact upon our capacity to be happy.

Globally, the situation is much the same. In developing their Democratic nomination campaigns for the 2020 US presidential election, candidates had been appealing to the young in terms of finances. Bernie Sanders said that he intended to wipe student debt. The economic climate has taken a real dip since the baby boomer generation were young. Democratic presidential hopeful Bernie Sanders tweeted:

The Boomer generation needed just 306 hours of minimum wage work to pay for four years of public college. Millennials need 4,459. The economy today is rigged against working people and young people.[9]

It can be hard for previous generations to fully comprehend the battle that today's young fight in order to be financially buoyant. The expectation of previous generations was that a job was a right and a house was within your reach. As Sanders' rival candidate Elizabeth Warren said:

We're crushing an entire generation with student loan debt and the consequences are everywhere. Young people can't buy homes. They can't start businesses. No country builds a future by crushing the dreams and hopes of its young people.[10]

Some countries' poor are in such difficult circumstances that they have had to come up with radical solutions to finding

9   Bernie Sanders, Twitter, 24 April 2019. Available at: https://twitter.com/berniesanders/status/1121058539634593794?lang=en.
10 Quoted in The Real News Network, Sanders & Warren Pitch Rival Plans to Address $1.6 Trillion in Student Debt (27 June 2019). Available at: https://therealnews.com/stories/sanders-warren-pitch-rival-plans-to-address-1-6-trillion-in-student-debt.

ways out of poverty. The Grameen Bank started up in Bangladesh in 1976, on the back of work by Professor Muhammad Yunus at the University of Chittagong. Yunus launched a research project to study how to make credit available to the rural poor. The bank is committed to making collateral-free loans to enable the poor to become self-employed. This fosters the important notion of workers as job creators rather than job seekers. Can you provide a service that is newly created or that did not previously exist? The idea of job creators will trigger genuine movement in the job market.

There are still, however, plenty of roles that require qualifications. To get qualified, you have to go to university. The way in which the burden of university tuition fees has moved from the taxpayer/government to students has meant that young graduates are saddled with crippling debt. Once you leave university, you have a degree that might in previous years have meant that you were pretty much guaranteed a good job. However, there has been a huge rise in the number of people attending university and gaining a degree. In 1980, 68,150 undergraduate degrees were awarded at UK universities. By 2011, that figure had risen to 350,800.[11] If, as was the case for me in 1984, only one in twenty people were getting a degree, being in that minority meant I had an advantage in seeking a job. The numbers attending have since vastly increased, and the advantage that I had is no longer the case. In 2017, 32.6% of 18-year-olds were accepted onto university courses.[12]

'Yeah, I've got a degree, but it's not been much help in what I do or in finding work ... a 2:1 isn't what it used to be.'

11 Paul Bolton, *Education: Historical Statistics*. Ref: SN/SG/4252, House of Commons Library (27 November 2012), p. 20.
12 UCAS, Largest Ever Proportion of UK's 18 Year Olds Entered Higher Education in 2017, UCAS Data Reveals (27 November 2017). Available at: https://www.ucas.com/corporate/news-and-key-documents/news/largest-ever-proportion-uks-18-year-olds-entered-higher-education-2017-ucas-data-reveals.

What you are guaranteed today is a mountain of debt. The fees and loans are not really fees and loans at all; they are a form of income tax. Debts can generally be in the range of £50,000, with students from poorer backgrounds having debts that are higher still. Having this hanging over you once you leave university is debilitating. It stops people from making even cautious monetary decisions about investing in starting a business.

Further still, some families are proud to have never owed anything to anyone and they have earned every penny that crossed their hands. To them, the whole idea of carrying debt is completely at odds with how they conduct themselves. This is a genuine stumbling block, preventing some people from even entering higher education. Huge debt is not something that should be taken on lightly. If it is, it can quickly seem like a normal way to conduct both your personal and business finances.

'Top jobs are all rigged anyway. I'm from the East Midlands and went to a normal school … you'd need to have been to Eton and have Daddy getting you the post for most of the real top jobs.'

Andrew Grice, writing in *The Independent* back in May 2012 after Alan Milburn – the coalition government's independent adviser on social mobility and child poverty – revealed some rather damning insights, agrees with my interviewee:

Today, although only 7 per cent of people are educated at private schools, they still have a "stranglehold" on the top professional jobs, Mr Milburn said. The "forgotten middle class" as well as those at the very bottom of the ladder miss out because they lack the right connections. So the next generation in the professions will look very similar to today.[13]

The disadvantaged seem to stay disadvantaged as the privileged can look forward to the maintenance of the status quo. This is largely a case of the haves protecting what they have in these austere times. Our young are turning their backs on paid employment to have a go on their own terms. Schools need to be actively involved in supporting the young to understand how money works and how they can make sure that they are, as a first priority, economically healthy and, subsequently, able to develop their financial strategies. With (often expensive) credit, it is all too easy to buy things today and have no means to pay for them tomorrow. And with contactless payments, it is all too easy to lose track of what you are spending. We must help our children understand economics.

13 Andrew Grice, 'Unlock the Closed-Shop Professions', The Independent (31 May 2012). Available at: https://www.independent.co.uk/news/uk/politics/unlock-the-closed-shop-professions-7804981.html.

Chapter 5

HAPPINESS AND WELL-BEING

Is a bit of dissatisfaction a healthy thing? Is it natural for us to strive for a little, and sometimes a lot, more? Is a measure of frustration a motivating factor when we think about how to better our lives? Does not getting what you want too easily help as we strive to improve and innovate? Or is it purely greed? If it is greed, has it been fostered by the culture around us, driving us to want more and more material possessions? How do we judge being happy? What would you say if you were asked what makes you happy and whether you were happy or not? What evidence would you reach for to justify your answer?

'... officially click-happy ... marmite ... exciting knitwear ...'

Whilst it was evident that the young people who I interviewed were successful in terms of their work, I also wanted to find out if that success was translating into being happy. Do schools promote happiness was a question at the forefront of my mind as I was planning to write this book.[1] How could a school promote happiness? School inspections don't specifically go looking for this detail, relying instead on short passing references to well-being. It should be a key indicator of the success of a school. A head teacher should be able to

---

1   See Caron Carter, Is Friendship Something That Can Be Taught in Schools?, *Sheffield Hallam University* [blog] (31 October 2016). Available at: https://blogs.shu.ac.uk/sioe/2016/10/31/is-friendship-something-that-can-be-taught-in-schools-3/?doing_wp_cron=1564356381.8568780422210693359375.

tell me, or anyone else for that matter, the ways in which their school actively promotes the happiness of their children. It strikes me that schools do a lot of remedial work when children are clearly unhappy and their well-being is poor, but what do we do to promote well-being as a proactive choice? A choice is certainly how our successful young people think about happiness.

'I think that mental health is a choice. You have to buy into it. I think that you have to make sure that you leave some time for yourself. You need to look after yourself. One of the pressures that I have is that I get quite a lot of colds and things like that when I get run down. I often say to myself that I can't be ill because if I am off work then I am not getting paid. This can be a bit of a downward spiral. You have to look at leisure time as a loss-leader. You don't get paid for it, but it does hopefully mean that you are fresher when you are working. So it can make economic sense.'

In *Why Do I Need a Teacher When I've Got Google?*, Ian Gilbert discusses three types of happiness:

you can't buy your way to happiness … [bought happiness] is the most transitory type, happiness through relationships is the next best and happiness through having a meaning in your life comes out on top.[2]

Happiness can be short-term and instant, such as the short-lived high we get when we purchase material goods that we desire. Pursuing this kind of happiness can be addictive as

2   Ian Gilbert, *Why Do I Need a Teacher When I've Got Google?* (Abingdon: Routledge, 2011), p. 89.

the effect of the purchase wears off quickly, and this can actually lead to a good deal of harm. Happiness can also be a longer term feeling of satisfaction based more around a sense of well-being. There were many important things that the young people told me about happiness.

There are a number of ways in which they aspire to be happy. The most striking to me was the idea that a measure of happiness can be gained from feeling purposeful: that there is deep satisfaction to be found in feeling that you are making a positive and important contribution in some way. What a wonderful way to look at your work. This suggests that purpose can be felt; that it has an emotional significance. I like that. When we consider poor behaviour in school, I think that often the real cause is pupils feeling that what they are doing is pointless. We do need to be explicit about the ways in which what we do in the classroom has purpose and is meaningful. Purpose clearly creates a positive feeling.

Another significant theme was being able to, because you make sure it happens, make time for pleasure outside of work. The measurement here is time. Are there ways in which we can promote our students' understanding of a strong work–life balance? For instance, I think that we need to move away from organisers/planners that are in paper form. Diary appointments (the timetable/assemblies/clubs) can be kept in electronic form with alerts programmed in. Homework could be directly written in by teachers. That way, no one can say that they didn't write the homework down or know what lesson they had next. Children are always losing their planners. There is no chance that they are going to lose their phones as easily.

'Tuesday night is my night – I go to yoga and meet the girls. I always make a point of going out at least one night at the weekend as well.'

In often quite isolated occupations, having social contact is important. Often work meetings were conducted in bars and cafes. The young like to take their laptops to coffee houses and work there, specifically because they might meet up with friends and business contacts. But most were able to talk about how they plan their leisure time.

'Laughter is really important. You've got to have a laugh. It's about being with other people and enjoying their company. But you have to plan your leisure time in these days. If you don't make time each week that is yours then it will quickly get consumed by work ... you need to be able to tell yourself when enough is enough.'

The ability to travel also contributed to happiness. I think that the concept of travel has broadened with the younger generation. When they talk about the joy of being able to travel, they mean both with work and in the more conventional sense of holidaying. They enjoy having more than one job and the ways in which a job can be different every day. I think that the young are more careful to try to find work that suits them and that sustains their well-being. The percentage of interviewees who had had more than three jobs by the age of 20 was 45% and by 25 that had doubled to 90%.

'I measure success through three things really: travel, opportunities and experiences. I guess making money is also a big part of that, but I am not as likely to talk about that.'

A good number of the jobs undertaken were in order to sustain another more interesting but less secure aspiration.

'I left education two years ago and I have already had two paid jobs and am doing some work freelance as well. I am moving more towards the freelance. I think my mum is going to go mad ... she thinks I need to get a job and stick at it ... I don't think she understands the way it works anymore. In any case, I want a varied career path.'

The young would rather leave a job than be unhappy in that work. I think that this frame of mind is possible because of the way in which they now expect a work life in which they will take on many jobs over a lifetime.

'I'm pretty realistic about the fact that I might need to have more than one line of work. I keep looking at ways to diversify the things that I do now. You've got to keep up to date but you also have to have an eye on the future. It might be that what you do now suddenly isn't viable anymore. Look at the way photography has developed. There's not much money to be made from rolls of film anymore. But if you see something like that happening in your line of work, you've got to think about where you are going to take your expertise and experience next. That can make you anxious and it can seem like a negative drag on your energy, but I think you've got to do it.'

Being healthy and living healthily was also a measure of success for some. They generally had a good knowledge of physical well-being. There were a couple who would have the occasional cigarette in social situations but, on the whole, nobody would really class themselves as a smoker. A good number could describe quite rigorous dietary regimes that were clearly the source of some pride.

Having a partner was also a source of happiness for those who were in a relationship and a cause for some concern for those who were not. They all seemed to value a partner as someone to share your feelings with, as a sounding board and a confidante.

Having some wealth was also cited as a factor, although only in a quietly competitive way. A few of my interviewees suggested that it was nice to be making more money than their peers and people like them. Most professed to this as a quiet pleasure that they wouldn't share out loud too often!

Interestingly and hearteningly, the ability to keep learning was identified. To be able to nurture skills you already have and to develop new ones offered a good number of my interviewees a source of satisfaction.

> 'My mental health is good, good ... I'm on track to where I want to be with it. I wasn't always as happy with my life, my job ... I had to go to counselling ... I was surrounded by negativity, I got low and anxious and started making excuses for myself ... told myself, I'll settle for this ...'

But then again, there was a substantial flipside. Not all was well with our 'successful' young people. Can we contemplate success without happiness? Do you have to be successful to be happy? Surely, it should not be reduced to an either/or situation.

Amid discussion of a crisis in children's mental health, schools are ushering in a focus upon well-being. Peer relationship pressures, examination stress and the inability of some families to care for their children adequately are often named as contributing factors leading to a nation of unhappy young people. Media reports swing between sympathy for young people – and an understanding of the pressures that their generation are under – and calling them 'snowflakes', suggesting that they are helplessly falling without any capacity for resistance. We often hear resilience being proffered as an educational goal; however, making children and young people hardened to the difficulties of society seems like a last resort to me. First, we could try making society more amenable, and joining in easier.

In my interviews there were also signs of what is known as millennial burnout. This phrase describes a state of chronic stress that leads to physical and emotional exhaustion. The young people I spoke to variously described the following symptoms:

- An inability to relax. A number said that they just didn't know how to relax. Most had a to-do list that was hanging over them. This can come with the territory when you are self-employed and need to know where the next opportunity is going to come from.

- Being hyper-alert, leading to stress, anxiety, depression and sleep deprivation. Being hyper-alert is about not missing that chance to forward your business and your profile. You need to be constantly checking emails and direct messages. When there are any prolonged periods of inactivity in terms of getting new jobs and projects, anxiety and depression can quickly take hold.

- A number confessed to comparing themselves unfavourably to others around them in terms of their abilities. Again, here we have another reason why our young people would benefit if schools planned to build confidence. A healthy outlook was described as 'you are only in competition with yourself'. Whilst this is better, it still puts pressure on the individual.

- Stress around being expected to be constantly available. This creates that need to be online all the time and causes people to constantly overcommit, causing issues with deadlines not being met or having to stay up all night to meet the needs of a project.

- There was some discussion of errand paralysis, in which even the most minor of jobs begins to seem impossible. Once you get overwhelmed with the number of things on a to-do list, then getting any of them done seems like an almost impossible task.

- Many of my interviewees suggested that their job was too big a priority. This leads to a good deal of self-pressure to work hard, to the exclusion of having time for friends and family commitments.

- There is a new idea around success that is perhaps narrowing choice. To be a success in your work, and in your life, you need to have a fashionable job. You also need to be doing all the fashionable lifestyle things: hitting the gym at 5 a.m., finding time for street food and getting onto the guest list for festivals and events.

As mentioned previously, my interviewees were clear that they do see well-being as a choice, or at least as something over which they have agency. They see it as something that has to be worked at and that it has the potential to disappear any minute. It's not going to just happen; you have to make it happen.

They measure success in all sorts of ways. The chance to be creative is one that recurs: having a career in which you get to express yourself is highly valued. These young people are determined to have jobs and careers that they feel suit them. Having opportunities to seek unique experiences is another important measure of success. The young have not entirely let go of the idea of owning a home, although this is a dream that they hope to realise in their thirties, rather than a more immediate goal. The subject of money was treated in a quieter way. I got the general impression that young people see having money as a volatile situation. There was a good deal of reserving it for a rainy day. There was a good deal of suspicion of banks and financing. Young people want money to help them 'grow' and live a comfortable lifestyle, and to promote their sense of happiness. Additionally, a good number of interviewees indicated the importance of feeling that they have control over their own fate.

'It's not easy but it's important to look after yourself ... I won't sponge off my mum.'

I asked each interviewee to rate themselves on a scale of 1 to 10 (10 being the highest) as to how successful they feel. Answers ranged from 4 to 9. Those at the lower end of the range seemed to me to have very challenging expectations of themselves and they were often using longer term markers of success. Those who rated themselves higher tended to have shorter term aspirations that they could see their way towards more immediately. Being able to see ways forward was a feature of the conversations that I had. All of the interviewees were able to talk about the next steps that they felt would move them in the direction they wanted to go.

So happiness is characterised by my young interviewees as a feeling of purposefulness, being able to make time for leisure and relaxation, having social contact, being able to afford travel, having a partner, having some money in your pocket, being healthy and being able to have new experiences and keep learning. Is this any different from what the last generation hoped for? I suspect not. Are these things more difficult to achieve? I suspect that they might be.

However, one advantage they do have is that they also find pleasure in just being young. They recognise that they have the benefits of being fit, being healthy, having options, lacking ties and having a world of opportunity ahead of them, without the need for too much of a plan. There is joy to be found in facing the world with a fresh optimism and a can-do attitude that is resistant to knocks and bumps, and that gets up fighting again if it does fall.

Future school III

Today I am attending my weekly tutor meeting around my well-being. I have to attend at least one a week but can go to all four if I need them. I have emailed ahead and arranged to meet my tutor at the student services building in town. I have had a good look through my portfolio before attending.

I want to check my academic progress against the records that my tutor has been sent from the Lumilo glasses reports from my teachers.[3] I have the option of attending lessons, with teachers facilitating learning rather than delivering the content. My tutor has been given the feedback from the lesson I attended at the laboratory downtown and from the study session I took with them, which I attended in the library. I would like to look at the ways in which I am building my portfolio, the file with which I will leave school that demonstrates what I have achieved and the skills I have been building. It is also a cloud repository for me of all the materials I have decided to save as a library. It records my general reading age/level and the

---

3   Lumilo AR glasses are smart glasses for teachers that are being trialled in pilot schools by Carnegie Mellon University in Pittsburgh. Whilst pupils are working with their own individual AI tutoring systems, if the teacher hovers their gaze through the glasses directly over the pupil, performance indicators are made visible above the pupil's head. If the pupil is making lots of errors or doing well, being idle or cheating, the glasses can give immediate feedback to the teacher. The records are also able to be stored for later use. In the pilot, evidence is being gathered which suggests that pupils' performance is going up and that teachers are able to direct their support more efficiently where it is needed. This resource was generated from asking teachers the question, 'What teacher superpowers would you like to have?' Answers were about being able to see how learning is taking place, how patterns of mistakes are forming and how nervous or confident students are, and having an insight into the general performance of the class as a group. Lumilo glasses have the capacity to make a teacher's life so much easier. For more information, see: https://kenholstein.myportfolio.com/the-lumilo-project.

level of challenge in the actual reading that I have under-taken. The annotated copies of the texts that I have worked with are also collected in my online library. I will be able to keep this record fully intact as I go out into the real world of work and as I continue my lifelong learning journey.

My attendance and engagement records are good. I am going to gain enough credit to pass the arts project at strength level. (There are three levels: competence, strength and expertise.) The chip embedded between the finger and thumb of my right hand has sent health records to my portfolio. It notes that it is time for a couple of inoculations. It has also uploaded details of how much of the food/drink subsidy I have used this month and the relative strength of my health indicators. The virus checker has given me a clean bill of health for my online life. In my inbox, there are some interesting suggestions for contacts and information relating to our project about saving the bees. I will make time to check these.

My well-being is also covered by my portfolio. In there are my medical records since birth. My heart rate and other basic physiological outputs are monitored and recorded. The dates of my regular check-up appoint-ments are noted and the portfolio is able to monitor my sleep patterns and associated heart rate patterns.

Chapter 6
RELATIONSHIPS

The young are often viewed with suspicion by the old, as if there is something wrong with or dangerous about them.[1] However, the truth is far removed from this perception. Young people are, anecdotally, more likely to be accepting of diversity, equally likely to volunteer in formal ways and much more likely to volunteer in informal ways than their elders are. The young are free with their advice to friends, more likely to keep in touch with someone who they know is struggling, more likely to offer a lift to someone they know, more likely to look after a pet for someone and far more likely to babysit for someone. The young are just more open to things: willing to give it a go and to try to help. They are more accepting of your music choice, gender identity, sexual orientation and skin colour.

Young people talk about their 'story' and want to know about your 'story'. It is a plea for authenticity, a cry for the truth in this post-truth world. The expression 'story' in this use is straight from Instagram. But the sense that you have a story to tell is important: it is key to your ability to connect with others and believe that others will be interested in that story.

This is one topic that cropped up a lot: personal relationships. There was a general belief that having close relationships would, or does, have a negative impact on the business goals that you want to pursue. Interestingly, this pattern of response ran parallel to the understanding that feeling isolated and lonely was debilitating. As detailed previously, one of the sources of happiness that they identified is having a partner

---

1   There are some lovely sequences on this topic in *The War on the Old* (2016) and *The War on the Young* (2018) by John Sutherland (London: Biteback Publishing).

to share life with. Whilst most could see that these arguments ran contrary to each other, nevertheless they held them both to be true.

> **'People slow you down. I don't have time for a relationship … I don't keep the hours for it.'**

Collaboration with colleagues seemed to be the main way into meeting people with whom you could socialise. Healthy business relationships lead to social relationships. Talking about work was a large part of this socialising and in some ways the socialising described to me was like an extension of work. A good deal of the networking that I observed was extremely relaxed and looked a lot like leisure. But these personal connections were building the foundations for trusting business relationships: the young buy into people as much as the product. If the person is 'sound', then the assumption is that the product will also be 'sound'.

The young don't cast off their school friends as much these days, particularly as we are now able to keep up with people's lives on Facebook and the like. The last generation of university graduates or relocators found it harder to know where their school friends were and what they were up to once they had moved on from their hometown. On the other hand, Facebook has the distancing effect of not having to call or physically meet up with someone to know what they are doing. Keeping in touch can be reduced to a few short messages or likes.

What role should schools play in the development of children's personal lives as they move towards adulthood? Do our teachers have the necessary understanding of how relationships are forged in the 21st century to offer useful advice and counsel?

Indeed, research points to the idea that the 'family' needs to be moved from its central position as the basic unit of relationships in the 21st century. Sasha Roseneil and Shelley Budgeon write:

We recognize that the idea of 'family' retains an almost unparalleled ability to move people, both emotionally and politically. However, much that matters to people in terms of intimacy and care increasingly takes place beyond the 'family', between partners who are not living together 'as family', and within networks of friends.[2]

'It's always good to meet with clients and with colleagues but I really couldn't mix those friendships with any kind of relationship.'

How do you make friends in the 21st century? Where are you going to find a partner? If you look online, how do you know if someone is who they say they are, or even if they are a real person? How can you form proper adult relationships when you live at home with your parents? How do you present yourself to an expectant world? How can you make friends when you are constantly 'at work' because you have to be online and available?

'I have about 500 Facebook friends and I probably see about 10.'

2   Sasha Roseneil and Shelley Budgeon, Cultures of Intimacy and Care Beyond
    'the Family': Personal Life and Social Change in the Early 21st Century,
    Current Sociology, 52(2) (2014)· 135–159 at 135. Available at: https://www.
    researchgate.net/publication/249680246_Cultures_of_Intimacy_and_Care_
    Beyond_the_Family_Personal_Life_and_Social_Change_in_the_Early_21st_
    Century.

The only contribution – that I can think of – that schools have made regarding the topic of relationships is around sex education, and that's only because it's a mandatory requirement. When you contemplate the harrowing and vaguely ridiculous sex ed lessons that you likely received at school, in what ways were these preparation for developing and nurturing adult relationships? When I think back to that 'curriculum', either as a pupil or as a teacher, I am left halfway between a laugh and a tear. Dear oh dear, how underwhelming. In the age of loneliness, we are going to have to do better than the condom-on-a-banana trick! If the young are going to be working in greater isolation, we are going to have to support their understanding of how to find and look after their friendships.

> **'I can't be pregnant … I just can't. There is no time for a baby.'**

Schools are beginning to think about well-being and mental health, but in largely remedial ways. There is an understanding, in the development of schemes such as mental health awareness and trauma-informed schools, that children bring all sorts of issues into school with them. It is hard to concentrate on flood plains in geography or the rules of hockey in PE if you are starving hungry and you don't know where you are going 'home' to that evening. Our work around well-being tends to come when a problem is identified. Can we bring this forward to anticipate problems? Can that work include a focus upon building positive relationships?

'I've always got my school friends but making new friends is hard. I have always been pretty sociable but when you are flying in and out of places you never get to know anyone ... you're just not around anyone enough to forge a friendship.'

As Natalie Gil wrote in 2014:

The Mental Health Foundation found loneliness to be a greater concern among young people than the elderly. The 18 to 34-year-olds surveyed were more likely to feel lonely often, to worry about feeling alone and to feel depressed because of loneliness than the over-55s.[3]

When the young reach the age of 18, they become too old to access youth services. Provision for the young to talk about their problems is scant. The shiny, and largely false, social media posts that show friends 'living their best life' can persuade the young to keep quiet, feeling inferior. This leads to brooding on problems on your own.

A significant relationship that was mentioned over and over again was with someone who believed in them. The sense that another person was investing their time and friendship in my young interviewees made for a truly important relationship. Some of them mentioned their parents and siblings. However, just as prevalent were teachers, employers and social workers. Showing an interest in a young person can be the most important thing that you do as an educator. Long after the child has forgotten the education that you offered

---

3   Natalie Gil, Loneliness: A Silent Plague That Is Hurting Young People Most, *The Guardian* (20 July 2014). Available at: https://www.theguardian.com/lifeandstyle/2014/jul/20/loneliness-britains-silent-plague-hurts-young-people-most.

them, they will remember your kindness and they will remember the times when you truly listened and took their side. This kind of relationship can have a profound impact on the way in which the child acts as an adult.

In developing a strong character there are a number of foundational elements that need to be in place:

- At a survival level, you need clean air, clean water, enough food and shelter.
- You need to feel that you are safe and secure (this must apply in the classroom too).
- Your social needs are met through healthy and strong relationships with your family and friends.

If these needs are met then a person can become confident, leading to the raising of their self-esteem and hopefully to achieving the things that they set out to accomplish. The sense of worth that a person gets from these foundational supports can lead to them being able to enjoy a sense of self-actualisation. This is where the capacity to be creative, spontaneous and a problem-solver exists. In the next chapter we'll see how to build this foundation. Strong relationships are at the very centre of this chain of circumstances.

'I couldn't have told her back then, but my form teacher was the one who kept me in school. I never told her about all the doubters in my life ... and she never asked ... but she just kept faith in me, whatever I did. She must have seen something good in me, and I should thank her for that. In fact, I'm going to now I've thought about it.'

Chapter 7

DEVELOPING TALENTS

Some things about an education should remain timeless. Certain things are intrinsic to preparation for lives well-lived: the pursuit and appreciation of beauty; the development of self-awareness; and the understanding of what it means, and how, to be engaged and civil citizens. It is important that we can understand the needs of our environment and that we choose to feed ourselves wisely. We need to know how to stay healthy and we need to be kind to each other. We need to be able to speak up when we have something to say and we need to listen to others with empathy.

However, the ways in which we interact with the world around us are changing faster than we have ever had to deal with before. In expressing themselves through music, for instance, the young can watch YouTube tutorials in playing instruments, record their music using their laptops and upload it to Spotify, reaching a potential audience of millions around the world without any need for expensive music lessons and recording studio fees or a recording contract. The young can share their poetry online, and attend and contribute to spoken word events. If there isn't an event happening nearby, they can search the internet to find fellow artists and start the event themselves. The young can share photographs and videos on TikTok, Instagram and many other platforms. They can apply filters to the images and edit them to show their creativity. Our young people don't have to wait to find an audience; they are already artists, writers, speakers and creators.

Our education system is not coping with the seismic changes taking place all around us. The world and the ways in which each one of us can engage with it is beyond the scope of thinking even just fifty years ago. And yet our education system remains largely unchanged, lumbering on with a misplaced sense of security in the certainty of knowledge and the value of testing what can be remembered. Information has become overwhelming and is less trustworthy over new mediums. It is easy to be manipulated with 'soft facts'. We owe our children an education that is useful preparation for those 'timeless' aspects that we have now come to view so differently. Our children need a better explanation.

At the How the Light Gets In festival in London in September 2019, Stanley Fish, Howard Jacobson and Minna Salami debated the following topic:

There has always been dispute over which ideas are most significant. But at least there used to be broad agreement about the hallmarks of quality and the great works in each field. Now from literature to the social sciences there are claims that previous standards were structures of prejudice and oppression and calls are heard for greater inclusion.

How do we navigate this new space where there is so little agreement on merit? Should the origins of ideas matter as much as their substance? Should we even abandon the notion of 'great works' altogether, or would this threaten the very survival of our culture and much that we hold to be valuable?

Listening to this debate it struck me just how out of touch the older generations are with the millennial generation of creators and innovators. This is in large part because of the faith that the older generations have in the cultural capital of school education. There is a belief, or perhaps it's just an assumption, that pupils recognise the validity of the canon of literature and that they accept the science that they are offered as being up-to-date. Our pupils do not believe that school 'knowledge' is authoritative. What is 'learnt' in school is constantly being updated and disproved, the results of which are quickly disseminated online. School learning is just too slow, and the pupils know it. Even if they didn't, we should have the responsibility to keep the curriculum up to date and to not treat knowledge as if it's completely immovable. The rate of change, and the very fact that there is such high-speed change, needs to be given credence.

'ICT at school seemed decent, but as soon as I needed the skills I'd learnt, I found that what I knew was out of date.'

Our creative young people are looking for originality in their work. This is exacerbated by the fact that more and more people have the capacity to create, and have their creations be seen and heard. Anyone can take a photograph and publish it online now. The ability to record and disseminate music is fairly democratic; musicians do not need to have a record deal to have thousands of people listening to their music. A young writer can blog online and reach a huge audience. Sometimes the simplest of posts go viral on social media.

What kids know is just not important in comparison with whether they can think.[1]

'I'm a bright human being. I dropped out of sixth form ... was stubborn about doing it, but it wasn't for me. Now I need to prove to everyone that I'm not a failure.'

1   Mitra, *Beyond the Hole in the Wall*, loc. 59.

I have always been very wary of the expression 'gifted and talented'. As a teacher, I saw it as my responsibility to find the talent in all of my pupils and to try to bolster their confidence through the enthusiasm and encouragement that I have shown them – that was a key part of the work. Surely everyone has gifts and some go on to demonstrate those gifts through their talent. If we seek out those gifts and offer a forum in which the talent can be nurtured and showcased, then young people can feel positive about exploring their hopes and dreams. Every single one of your pupils must feel this way; we all have a talent to offer.

Sometimes schools exclude pupils' talents and interests because they don't fall within the narrow set of acumen sought by the curriculum.[2] The curriculum generally measures academic intelligence through the lens of the ability to follow the conventions of exam-answering: being able to read the question, the luck of the multiple-choice answer, the ability to write an academic essay, etc. Where and how do we measure or promote practical intelligence, emotional intelligence or physical intelligence? Why do we promote the idea that English, mathematics and science are in some way more important than the other subjects? In the case of English, and of being articulate in particular, the importance of physical writing and grammatical knowledge is about to take a big nosedive. AI machines will do your writing for you soon: you will speak to your device and once you have completed 'writing' your text, you can request any language you want and the grammar will also be attended to for you! We are conquering illiteracy in writing by handing it over to machines.

There are a number of trends that came across in the interviews which indicate how learning is really being achieved as

---

2   The curriculum is narrow in the sense that it only looks for 'academic intelligence' but is also being narrowed to an all-encompassing set of preparations for exams. NAHT, Schools Are 'Narrowing' the Curriculum, Says Ofsted (30 November 2017). Available at: https://www.naht.org.uk/news-and-opinion/news/curriculum-and-assessment-news/schools-are-narrowing-the-curriculum-says-ofsted/.

these young people continue to develop their talents in their working lives.

'I love to play around with ideas. School never seemed to let you do that; it was more about writing down the right answers. I think that is an unrealistic way to learn ... jumping straight from a question to the right answer misses out all the thinking and the chance to see if you can find other ways of solving the problem.'

There was a good deal of enthusiasm for the use of technology in developing their talents. Young designers and creators rely on software packages and assistants.

I recently made a short film called 'The Only Fresh Air Is Outside in the Yard'.[3] It documents the experience of a boy who is getting very little out of school. A part of that film, shot up on the moors between Baslow and Sheffield, was made with the benefit of a drone camera. Having been able to see at first hand just how easy it is to operate such a sophisticated piece of equipment, and having been able to see the potential that it offers, I am confident that making use of a drone could really open up thinking and creativity across the curriculum. Think about how you might use a drone to support your lessons. Don't put up the barrier of cost; think about how you might stretch your pupils, how you might hook in engagement. Drones for classroom use are becoming a possibility as the price falls.

A prevalent learning model discussed during the interviews and endorsed by the young people was that of looking at 'greatness' or 'quality': by this, I mean researching, getting to see and learning from examples of work that you admire. Those pupils who are engaged, those whose curiosity has

3   See https://www.youtube.com/watch?v=A7mj7Y7sx_l.

been sparked, are most likely to become invested in their learning. They are inspired by the wonder of mastery. Working with experts, watching what they do and listening to their advice is a popular way of developing talent. As mentioned elsewhere, the experts admired by my interviewees tended to be very young themselves.

> 'Standing and watching him play is inspirational ... listening to him talk, even better.'

On the other hand, unpicking and improving upon work that you think is poor was another model for developing talent that I was offered. It makes sense to look at what has been done before to find ways in which you could do better.

Time for theoretical learning was difficult to find and many said that the development of talent usually happened in the immediate needs of everyday solution-finding – learning 'on the job'. A problem presents itself and it needs sorting straightaway. New developments and new ways of thinking also offer the opportunity to experiment, as do new pieces of equipment. My interviewees recognised the importance of keeping interested and trying new things as a way to develop their talents.

I spoke to a number of young people from the creative industries who frequently go looking for opportunities to work and learn in their local community. They also try to make use of the environment around them. Talking to people who are interested in your field of work can spark your creativity. Working in different places can have the same effect.

'I noticed the skateboard scene first but there's a whole other scene going on down there ... film-makers, musicians, tattooists, fashion stuff ... they're all down there ... loads of collabs going on.'

In my work as a teacher I always try to encourage what I call 'noticefulness'. Can we get pupils being observant about the landscape around them? Could you ask them to photograph something beautiful, or an interesting street sign, or something they've never noticed before on the way home?

All our children have talents. Our job is to spot those talents, encourage them and support children to think positively about their abilities and interests. Being a great fisherman might result in many years of recreational pleasure or it might lead to fulfilling work in the fisheries industry. Whatever it ends up amounting to, a teacher's interest in that child's love of fishing will support their confidence and self-esteem.

The camera is an instrument that teaches people how to see without a camera.

Dorothea Lange[4]

One feature of the mobile phone that our young rely on a lot is the camera. Let the customer see your product, let the customer see you. Shape and frame your images so that you get your website and your social media right. Apply filters and crop the images. Enhance the text and sound. The young are alive to the possibilities of visual impressions. Alongside the photograph taken to document aspects of your business, there is the social photograph: the selfie, the speaking to camera video and the everyday image of life.

4   Quoted in Milton Meltzer, *Dorothea Lange: A Photographer's Life* (Syracuse, NY: Syracuse University Press, 2000 [1978]), p. vii.

Our young people are growing up in a new era for photography. They don't recognise it as new; to them it's just natural. But, nonetheless, it is new. Once the domain of the expert, it has become the way in which everyone[5] tells the story of their lives. These photographs are less about art or documentation; this new social photography is more about communication. It is a form of storytelling. Photographs appear in streams rather than in isolation as users add to their profiles and stories. There is a general understanding that these photographs are ephemeral. It is less about committing the present to memory so that in the future you can remember the past, and more about marking the present here and now. The photos provide a running commentary of our lives.

Not so long ago you could go weeks without taking a photo. That is unheard of in our young. The networked community/audience creates the motivation.

'I spend a good deal of time making sure my images look good. People are looking more than they are reading, I promise you.'

Our young people are learning to manipulate this new facility for creating images and memories that might otherwise go unheeded. The availability and ubiquity of the camera allows for active observation. The camera allows us to document those things that we have spotted and wish to share. The camera, always in your pocket, affords the opportunity and motivation to communicate. Understanding that potential can be the key to having a strong online presence.

Elly Lucas is a professional photographer who lives in and works out of Sheffield. She has always been very musical. At school, her GCSE presentation to the class was entitled 'Musical me' and involved her playing seven different folk

---

5 Okay, so perhaps you or someone you know is not on social media or taking photos in this way, but the young certainly are, in overwhelming numbers.

instruments. As part of the duo David Gibb & Elly Lucas, she was nominated for the BBC Radio 2 Young Folk Award in 2011. Her life has also thrown up many challenges and her mental strength has been tested beyond that which most young people have to endure. But she is a fabulously strong person, having developed a keen eye for reflection.

Elly has combined her love of photography and folk music. Many of the images on the album covers, posters and Spotify pages of folk musicians that you might know have been taken by Elly. She has made a niche for herself and she is now so in demand that she has been able to drop the wedding photography service that she initially offered whilst she set up her music photography business. She is now working full-time in the field that she loves.

She has a lively online presence: a mix of talk to camera and examples of the stunning photographs that she takes of nature and of the musicians with whom she works. Elly is able to talk about her expertise and passion for creating images, text and sound with great clarity of purpose. In this Instagram post she discusses the cathartic nature of the creative process:

'I've been enjoying the challenge of creating additional snapshots without the use of my camera recently; of absorbing as much sensory information as I can and deciding upon an alternative means of articulating my findings. Sometimes these involve a multitude of words; sitting quietly, taking a deep breath and challenging myself to capture the moment in pen and ink and as much detail as I can muster. Other times, particularly times of overwhelming emotion or bewildering nothingness, the necessary words can feel light years beyond my reach – but I find something else dancing towards my fingertips. This musical reaction isn't always especially refined or as theoretically articulate, I still feel like I've a long way to go when it comes to the technical aspects of my playing, but it is always honest. It might not describe minutiae – I'm perpetually in awe of composers and players who can weave such rich images from sound – but it still (to me) describes the moment.'[6]

Elly recently worked with folk and crossover musician Ralph McTell, famous for his song 'Streets of London'. Her photographs of McTell began to appear across mainstream media platforms in August 2019. She commented on Instagram about how this is an important step forward for her personally, but also something that validates what she has chosen to do.

'I mean, I personally get pretty giddy when any of my images of the wonderful people I work with start appearing like this (BBC Radio 2 website), but it is extra lovely when my not-particularly-folky relatives immediately get excited about this too. I bailed out of my AS levels to run off and take photos and play music and, while they were very supportive, it was definitely a cause of worry to them for a while – so moments like this do feel extra special.'[7]

6   Elly Lucas, Instagram, 6 August 2019. Available at: https://www.instagram.com/p/B00JU7bBvkK/.
7   Elly Lucas, Instagram story, 22 August 2019.

Future school IV

I am now what I like to call a 'barista plus'. I have been hired because I can do the social media networking and promotion for the cafe. It's a job that I am developing myself. I schedule in images on Instagram of the range of coffees and cakes, the people who work here and the local businesses in the units around our cafe. It seems to be generating a real buzz and the cafe is becoming a bit of a hub. I still make and serve coffee, but I also think that I have made myself indispensable. The social media output is creating a scene around the cafe and it is definitely the place to be. And it is attracting the people that we want here. Wi-Fi and latte is the new office space and we are pretty much at the forefront of inviting these people in. Sales are going up and there is a real momentum about the place. Other staff are feeling emboldened too. They are making serving suggestions and we have branched out in the range of cakes that we offer: we've got the vegetarians and vegans covered. We've got gluten- and nut-free options. You have to keep an eye out for the changing tastes and attitudes of the customers. You need to keep changing the menu: people want the old favourites but they also want to try something new. One of the businesses across the way has offered me a job running their social media. It's more money and it's a full-time post. Perhaps it's no more coffee-making for me.

With my other jobs – hosting the Monday night open mic sessions at a local club and helping to set up events at a recording studio – I am doing alright. It's all part of me making money and being involved in the music industry. I seem to be receiving some good attention for my music on Spotify, and one or two music-business people have come down to see me play. The jobs I have are pretty flexible about when I'm there and how much I do. That allows me time and space to pursue the music. I am gaining good experience about how the music industry works and learning how to promote myself. I am developing a strong network of musicians locally and have found a few who I want to record and tour with. I think that it might just come together.

. . . .

Businesses have begun to eye top grades in school examinations with a measure of suspicion. Does a set of excellent results really suggest an enquiring mind? Is it more likely that the pupil has learnt the skill of doing what they are told? Does the exam system as it stands promote the skills that businesses profess to need? Confident decision-making, emergent problem-solving and creativity are low down on the list of competencies that are tested in our school examinations.

Young people have come to understand the needs of our rapidly changing world and are thinking about how they can join in. Increasingly, they know the importance of learning. But the nature of what is to be learnt and the value of that learning is evolving quickly. More and more, the young value, and society needs, short-term, specific skill sets. I say short-term because the rate of change will dictate that, once learnt, skills will quickly need to be updated and amended – we can't say that the learning is finished. The young want the skills but are far less likely to need the piece of paper that says they can do something, so online courses and non-traditional settings become important bases for learning.

Even if you are looking for a more traditional salaried role with an employer, there is a new respect for experience that hasn't been gained through the traditional university route. In a blog post, the US recruitment company Glassdoor listed fifteen companies that will hire you to a well-paid, secure job without a degree.[8] They include Google, Bank of America and Penguin Random House amongst their ranks.

None of us really know which areas of employment are going to thrive or be protected because of technological advances. We can reasonably estimate that most of the jobs that children who are in primary school now will go into do not yet exist. The World Economic Forum puts the number at 65%.[9]

The self-employed are the fastest growing demographic of our workforce. It is no longer reasonable to assume that if you do well in school and pass your exams that you will get a good job or, if you do, that you'll be ready for it. Learning is going to be a lifelong pursuit; the young people I interviewed recognise the need to keep learning and enhancing their skill sets. They are also learning that sometimes you have to start again and do things in a completely different way.

8   Glassdoor, 15 More Companies That No Longer Require a Degree – Apply Now (14 August 2018). Available at: https://blog-content. glassdoor.com/site-us/no-degree-required/.
9   World Economic Forum, *Future of Jobs Report: Employment, Skills and Workforce Strategy for the Fourth Industrial Revolution* (January 2016), p. 3. Available at: http://www3.weforum.org/docs/WEF_Future_of_ Jobs.pdf.

Chapter 8
MAKING DECISIONS AND BEING CREATIVE

Twenty-five years of neurobiological research tells us that children learn best when they feel loved.

Dr Andrew Curran[1]

We continue to be fascinated by the workings of the brain. Much of the recent neuroscientific research is focused on our ability to think. We are constantly making choices; it is a key part of our business and personal lives. One of the pieces of advice that my young interviewees had for children who will soon be leaving school and who hope to enter the adult world successfully was to be sure to do their best to make good choices.

In *Elastic: The Power of Flexible Thinking*, Leonard Mlodinow proposes that there are three types of thinking that the brain undertakes.[2] Firstly, there is the unconscious mode. This is, if you like, the thinking that our brains do for us. It is an autopilot system that regulates our responses and actions most of the time. The brain gathers data to create what is effectively a hard drive of information that it uses to allow us to make simple decisions without conscious thought. Your brain tells you that you need to move through the door without walking into the frame and when you have become adept at driving a car, most of the mechanical manoeuvres that you perform are done without conscious thought. It is a kind of shortcut to make most of life simple, or at least simpler.

---

1   See https://www.independentthinking.co.uk/associates/dr-andrew-curran/.
2   Leonard Mlodinow, *Elastic: The Power of Flexible Thinking* (London: Penguin, 2018).

Secondly, there is analytical thought. This is the type of thinking whereby you consciously work through a sequence of logical steps towards an answer. It is the type of thinking that is tested and rewarded in most school examinations. The brain moves through a process of logical sequencing from one idea to the next, guided by rules.

Most interestingly, is Mlodinow's third type of thinking: elastic thinking. This is when the brain gathers together a number of variables in order to problem-solve. We formulate and invent criteria with which to approach a situation. This is the type of thinking that best suits a world of constant change. If you stick to analytical thinking, as much of our curriculum demands that you do, then you will be pretty much stuck with the status quo. Elastic thinking opens up the possibility of looking forward and refining your sense of what is possible. It is also a type of thinking that I recognised in the responses of my interviewees when talking about their work.

> 'I have a way of thinking that I call the fourth way. With anything, there is what you want, what they want and a compromise somewhere in-between ... if I think that there might be some disagreement, I try to think of another way: the fourth way.'

I have already discussed how, in the coming years, people are going to have to reinvent themselves over and over again to meet the needs of new jobs, new technologies and new circumstances as our societies shift and adapt. We are going to need to go past rational, logical and analytical thought more and more. Generating ideas, balancing and reconciling diverse and opposing ideas, and having the imagination to conceive of things that don't yet exist are crucial skills. This kind of thinking links to creativity and imagination but also to confidence: we need to be self-assured enough to try things out.

'If there's one thing I can do it's make mistakes, but that's okay ... as long as you learn from them and change what you're doing.'

Making mistakes was something that most of my interviewees talked about. Some discussed them in really negative terms, telling me about the loss of time and money and how they had been set back by choosing the wrong options. However, most were reflective about mistake-making. Most saw it as an inevitable part of moving forward and most were also determined to make use of the mistakes by learning from them. I had one interesting conversation with a musician, in which we discussed how he had continued to play for free at events long after he needed to; his reputation had developed to the point where he should have been doing paid gigs. He was slowing down his capacity to make money. He reflected that what he learnt from this is that there are levels in the music industry and you have to notice when you have stepped up to the next one, and also that if you play for free then it can become an expectation. To not move on is a mistake in itself.

The sense that it is okay to make mistakes has, in part, fuelled the growth in 'project me' doers. Young people are, now more than ever, prepared to make mistakes and try things out. School is generally a poor breeding ground for creative and new thinking. I think that our curriculum needs to move away from its current model of looking at questions to which we already know the answer towards a more collaborative approach to solving problems to which the answer is yet to be discovered. This kind of approach would more closely mirror what is happening out in the real world.

Creativity was a common trait among the young people who I interviewed. In one of the activities that I conducted with them, I asked each participant to rate themselves against the following ten traits of people who are predisposed to being 'creative'. This list is adapted from the work of Tiffani Bova.[3]

Would you say that you:

- Easily become bored? (Although these days whenever anyone feels a little unoccupied it seems that they can always fill that boredom with Facebook or *FIFA*!)
- Are a risk-taker? (You are prepared to give things a go even though you aren't sure of a positive outcome.)
- Like to colour outside the lines? (You like making decisions independently and sometimes trying out things that are not 'officially approved', so to speak.)
- Think with your heart rather than your head? (Emotional intelligence, if you like.)
- Make lots of mistakes (not in a clumsy way)?
- Hate the rules? (Your hackles are up as soon as you are told that you have to do something, and do it in a certain way.)
- Prefer to work independently rather than as a team? (Although working in a team is fine, you'd rather get things done by yourself.)
- Change your mind a lot? (You take your time weighing up a decision, perhaps looking at a number of options.)
- Have a reputation for eccentricity? (People think you are a little mad sometimes!)
- Like to dream big? (Whether you leave the leg work to others or not, your vision is long term.)

Participants awarded themselves one point each time the answer was yes. The scores for my interviewees were generally very high. I think that what the ensuing conversations showed me was that this group of people have developed, or had within them, a genuinely independent spirit. This is a key

3   Tiffani Bova, Twitter, 31 January 2019. Available at: https://twitter.com/Tiffani_ Bova/status/1091088029832306688.

attribute, I think, in approaching the ever-changing world successfully. Increasingly, we are seeking problem-solvers and free-thinkers. Those who can dream up what we can achieve next will be the movers and shakers of the coming years.

The exam-focused model of education that still prevails is often dominated by the compulsion to get the right answer first time, every time. It strikes me that this is a very poor model of learning to offer children and lacks a dimension that is essential to real-world learning. You will make mistakes; how you deal with those mistakes and how you turn errors into positives is going to have a big bearing on your ability to see ways forward.

'My anxiety to get everything right started getting in the way at school … you end up focusing on what is required. What I have learnt from my work is that there are very few 'right' answers. Normally there are just options and you need to pick the best one.'

If you wanted to pursue a career as a musician in the 1970s, it was very much a dream that was out of reach for most young people. Most had nowhere to practise, no means of making a reasonable recording and no means of getting their music out to an audience.

At school you went to see the careers officer who told you what sort of work would suit you. It was never popstar/musician. Playing music and being in a band was a hobby – you needed to get a proper job. The concept sold to you was that you'd be doing that proper job for the rest of your life. You could play your music in your spare time.

But the world has changed and with it the attitude and expectations of the young. With technology has come access: to free instruction on how to play an instrument or record a song, to the recording software you can use at home and to the means of getting your music out to a worldwide audience without the involvement of a record company. Young people are increasingly prepared to take a day job whilst they chase what they really want to do. Musicians can work shifts in coffee shops whilst they hone their skills and make contacts, meaning that being a musician is a viable possibility.

> 'Being creative is cathartic. I love editing my photographs ... love always looking for a new perspective and playing with design features. It makes me happy.'

The creative process involves all manner of ways of thinking and of developing ideas. How can your curriculum respond to help young people work in creative and thoughtful ways?

- Making sure that our children see the potential of being bold and being brave. Young people need to be able to experiment with thoughts and concepts that seem bigger than they can imagine will succeed. Again, we must suggest that it would be okay if things don't work out first time or even at all. School can be a testing ground for ideas.

- Can we support children to develop a body of work that helps them to define and conceptualise their thinking? Science is constantly asking questions to which we don't yet have answers. In mathematics there are often many routes to the right answer and sometimes there is more than one answer. Sometimes we are still searching for an answer.

- In their chosen professions or enterprises, our children will need to go looking for their niche market. Can we support them to see the potential of different audiences?

- Can we support children in thinking about the value and purpose of things? Having a sense of purpose is connected to our sense of personal happiness. Can we ask plenty of 'Why?' and 'For what?' questions?

- Creativity is generated in the young when they are clear about the importance of the work that they are undertaking. This might be a sense of personal achievement or the belief that what they are doing really makes a difference to people's lives. Can we support them in thinking about the value that they can bring?

- In these days of instant gratification, can we help our students embrace the concept of success as a marathon not a sprint? Sometimes good things come to those who wait, are patient and play the long game. This could be a particular difficulty for this generation, who struggle with the need for immediacy and the impatience to keep achieving everything now.

- Can we help our children to see the difference between the surface attraction of things and the deeper merit of those things? Can we help them distinguish between marketing and creating?

- Where in the curriculum will you allow your students to test out their ideas? Ideas need moulding and redefining. Doing everything once and moving on will not develop this capacity in our children. We need to make time and space in the curriculum for trying things out.

- Will our children be able to develop an ability and a willingness to sacrifice some things so that they can achieve others? Will they have a willingness not to be too precious about their ideas?

Does your curriculum offer the opportunity to go past the analytical? Can you build in opportunities to problem-solve? Can you ask questions that don't have definite answers? Can you develop the power of the imagination?

'There's so much I don't know about the global markets for design work. I just keep developing my style and trying to build an online audience. The work's out there ... I am just having to find it.'

Information is one thing, but knowledge is another. Information is a set of facts and ideas. Knowledge is an understanding of the relationship between those facts. To be knowledgeable takes skill. In this AI- and internet-driven age, knowledge has become less stable. Knowledge is developing rapidly alongside the huge growth in information. This creates an imperative to keep up, and flexible thinking is a key skill in being able to cope with and respond to our ever-changing lives.

Chapter 9
ETHICS

Everywhere you look the beardy hipster culture is winning: start-up companies that are tech savvy and service orientated, independent retail stores offering vinyl and shabby chic clothing, street food vendors with dirty vegan junk food, retro everything, designer branding, graffitied art and grapefruit pale ale. The music scene is alive with open mic nights and the spoken word scene is buzzing with politics and self-expression. The revolution is urban and located in refurbished industrial buildings. The revolution is plastic-free and risk-aware. The revolution is bisexual, gender fluid and free to be what it wants. The revolution is made of celebrations, launch nights and after-parties. What a time to be young! And all of this is done with a social conscience that is all about the environment, about small local business togetherness and changing the world one individual at a time. It is an economically viable dropout!

'I'm living it now. You know, you won't get a revolution unless you ask for one. I'm on it.'

Whilst it has become part of the popular scene, I think that being ethical has really been pushed to the forefront of young people's consciousness because of the poor examples that previous generations have been setting. This is more than teen rebellion against parents, more than just a stance against the status quo. This is a revolution that is going to be televised, but no one is watching. There are many issues about which our young people want to have a say and they want to be heard. Don't be fooled by the television-anaesthetic-of-the-masses

Gogglebox. The young are not sitting at home watching the world on their televisions.

What are the big questions that we need to explore with our children? For instance, it is becoming clear that we are approaching a climate emergency that may well be beyond repair. What is it that we can actually do to attempt to save our planet and, in doing so, save ourselves?

Global warming – or, as the scientists and the young are beginning to call it, 'global heating' – is a priority. In March 2019, over 1.5 million people around the world marched in protest, rallying and organising online under #climatestrike. The numbers out on the streets were huge: 150,000 in Montreal, 40,000 in Paris, 100,000 in Milan, 30,000 in Brussels and 25,000 in Warsaw. @nowthisnews reported in March, 'Teens near Central Park in New York City as well as around the world are walking out of schools to call for more action on solving the climate crisis'.[1] The youth climate strike was started by Greta Thunberg. If the cause is big enough then the young are connected by the internet and can mobilise behind a 17-year-old girl whose story began with her protesting outside the Swedish parliament in August 2018. Her Twitter page has (as of February 2020) 4 million followers.[2] The internet has brought a generation together to create a powerful voice for change.

At Glastonbury in 2019, 93-year-old David Attenborough was applauded as a hero. He sees the attitude of the young towards saving the planet, according to an address he gave to parliament, as 'a source of great hope'. He continues, 'The most encouraging thing that I see, of course, is that the electors of tomorrow are already making themselves and their

1   @nowthisnews, Twitter, 15 March 2019. Available at: https://twitter.com/nowthisnews/status/1106620075631673345.
2   See https://twitter.com/GretaThunberg.

voices very, very clear.'[3] The young understand that the problem is coming their way.

The treatment of animals and their processing for meat or by-products like leather has led to a huge burst in interest in vegetarianism and, increasingly, veganism. Veganism has entered mainstream culture. Nearly a quarter of all new food patents are vegan. A high proportion of vegans are young people.[4] The young are becoming more particular about what they eat and are increasingly mindful about the packaging that their food comes in. They are against the unnecessary use of plastic and for recyclable and reusable materials.

In watching Trump's (said by many to be) racist presidency, built on walls (although the physical one on the southern border will never be built) and hatred, our young have a growing respect for the plight of the migrant. This is important as the migration that will be associated with worsening climate change will have an impact on how and where the world is populated. My interviewees could see the unrest that is caused by the fact that people feel excluded from British society in ways such as being unable to get a mortgage or a decently paid job. This has a knock-on effect for immigrants, as people look for someone to blame for their circumstances. Austerity breeds resentment and that resentment is often directed at the wrong people. The rich are getting richer; the poor, poorer. The chances of moving from the latter segment of society to the former are getting smaller and smaller. My interviewees rejected racism, seeing it as something that was largely in the past in terms of mainstream culture. They viewed the likes of the English Defence League (EDL) and UK Independence Party (UKIP) as cranks.

---

3 Peter Walker, David Attenborough: Polluting Planet May Become as Reviled as Slavery, *The Guardian* (9 July 2019). Available at: https://www.theguardian.com/tv-and-radio/2019/jul/09/david-attenborough-young-people-give-me-hope-on-environment.

4 Dan Hancox, The Unstoppable Rise of Veganism: How a Fringe Movement Went Mainstream, *The Guardian* (1 April 2018). Available at: https://www.theguardian.com/lifeandstyle/2018/apr/01/vegans-are-coming-millennials-health-climate-change-animal-welfare.

If the young people I spoke to were the only ones to vote, then the Labour Party would be in power with a strong majority, there might well be proportional representation, 16- and 17-year-olds would be voting and Nigel Farage would be in prison. Most of my interviewees vote with a definite swing to the left. Some write about politics and a small number had been on recent demonstrations, marches or political rallies. Their enthusiasm for Jeremy Corbyn is based on the perception that he is interested in the many rather than the rich few, which is much the same as the popular appeal that Bernie Sanders has in the US.

'You don't hear so much from Corbyn, but he's about everyone. He's not just in it for himself like the Tories are ... I think he cares.'

One issue that all my interviewees could agree upon was that of Brexit. There is huge support for Britain staying within Europe. Whilst all need to earn a wage through their own businesses or individual services, which might be affected by Britain's departure, their stance is based around the idea that moving away from Europe is a backward step. None believe that Britain should leave the European Union and they also believe that the great majority of their peers agree with them. I sensed a general feeling that 'the young' are a movement when it comes to voting: they are increasingly politicised and share views on key issues. They are in favour of sweeping away old-style politics.

'I can guarantee one thing that we [young people] will put right and that's Brexit. It will take us a lot less time to get us back into Europe than it is taking you lot to take us out.'

The young get their news online and are suspicious of and alert to biases in the media. This means that they see the huge protests in this country that are either scantily covered or not covered at all by traditional news outlets. On the whole, they don't watch television, and especially not for the news. There are many online communities that they can engage with which offer alternative views to those main-stream perspectives. Whilst it is true that they can be exposed to more extreme opinions on the internet, it is equally true that they will see a greater balance of perspectives. Young people are intensely interested in fairness. One of the ways in which our schools should be supporting pupils is in develop-ing a sense of healthy scepticism. They need to be aware of the potential for bias in what they read. They need to under-stand the motives behind the 'news' that they see.

Chapter 10
'QUALIFICATIONS'

Again from the philosophy and music festival How the Light Gets In 2019, here are some of the topics of the day. These are important discussions that indicate the ways in which we are having to deal with the rapid rate of change in society and how the provision of schooling is lagging behind.

- Are genetics more influential than we might wish to believe? Are parents deluded in imagining that upbringing and education are vital to their children's future success? Or do these studies and the apparent evidence risk leading us towards dangerous ways of thinking, cementing privilege for those with privileged backgrounds and worsening adversity and disadvantage?

- University education has long been seen as the route to personal and social progress. But critics now argue that the encouragement of higher education in those subjects that are largely irrelevant to working life is mistaken. Some go further, claiming that postgraduate degrees are little more than expensive pyramid schemes, raising university income whilst providing little or no value to the individual or to society as a whole.

- In the age of Wikipedia, should we give up on amassing knowledge as a measure of success? Do we need a radical rethink of our educational goals and how to reach them? Or are our universities rightly seen as great institutions and a global success story? (I'm not sure about the answer to the first two questions, but the answer to the third must surely be yes.)

Here is an anecdote about a brother and sister who took the eleven-plus exam in 1949 and 1950 respectively. The eldest, the brother, passed and went on to feel confident in his skills.

He got to go to grammar school and then on to university, eventually gaining an MA on top of his undergraduate degree. He made a good life for himself: progressing through his chosen career and ending up at the top of his profession. He retired early with an enhanced pension and bought a house abroad where he lives a very comfortable retirement. His sister also took the eleven-plus, but she did not pass and went to the local comprehensive school. There, the limits of her horizons were reined in and upon leaving school she took up a job working in a shelter for abused women and, later, a front of house role at the main offices of a big retail company. The whole of her life you would hear her saying that she wasn't clever, and occasionally adding that she had failed the eleven-plus. Both are now in their eighties.

If truth be told, the brother had passed the eleven-plus by one mark and the sister had failed by one mark. Whilst the gap is small and the difference negligible, the impact of drawing that line of success lasted a lifetime. We have a natural tendency to put a great deal of stock in the exam scores that we achieve, believing that the results are a measure of our worth. Whilst there are undoubtedly winners in an exam system, there are also built-in losers. If everyone did exceptionally then top results would cease to be so; they'd be average. The system needs people to fail. Everyone takes the same test regardless of the quality of teaching and preparation that they have had, regardless of their interests and aptitudes, regardless of the level of importance attached to education in their homes and regardless of the relevance of the tests to their varied lives. Schools are suffering under an immense pressure to produce strong exam results. This is a challenge that is almost impossible to achieve. In a comparative system, you have to have winners and losers.

The tests have also run their course. The ability to retain knowledge no longer makes sense as a measure of competence in a world overflowing with freely available information. Examinations need to go: they are no longer fit for purpose.

You don't like it, I don't like it, but we've got to do it. It's important … it's for the exam!

Most teachers at some point

There is a very evident decline in the authority given to traditional examinations. Our young people display a noticeable antipathy towards exams. The system needs to reclaim this authority if grades are to be trusted and considered worthwhile. In all honesty, young people want the learning but not the piece of paper. The ways in which teachers have gamed exams for well over a generation has demonstrated, to the young (and to teachers!), the limits to the value of the tests. What they want now is a new model of learning that is less about retaining and remembering and more about the capacity to find out on a need-to-know basis. This generation have found exams stressful, ridiculous and pointless, and they are now beginning to ignore the results.

'I was a good kid, so I tried my best with exams. I thought they were important at the time, but I can see that they don't tell you much about me … they were never really what I am … they were never personal to me.'

Young people will no longer define themselves by their exam results because they are all too alert to the fact that the retention of facts is a redundant skill.[1] They are also beginning to see that the exams are no longer about them. Exams are about measuring schools against each other. The emphasis has changed: when a pupil doesn't do well in a test, the thinking is now that the pupil has let the school down, not the other way around.

1   Watch the fabulous Suli Breaks on this topic: https://www.youtube.com/watch?v=D-eVF_G_p-Y.

'No, I don't really bother looking at qualifications – that won't tell you much. You're better off sitting them down, having a chat and seeing what sort of a portfolio they've got.'

So much of the nature of exam-taking was noted as being really unhelpful by my interviewees. It makes no sense to sit in an examination room in isolation with no sources of help. This is not how the world operates. Exams that are all about retaining information have become more difficult simply because no one retains information in their heads that way anymore. Memory is changing. The young are much better at retrieving information than they are at having it in their heads. Memory of facts has been outsourced to hard drives.

A more useful practice would be to assess the ability to locate and explore information by testing the way in which pupils approach unseen materials. This would be far closer to the real world set of skills that our young people will need.

'I'm not kidding, I have remembered nothing about geography ... nothing at all.'

Because the focus in our schools is so much on terminal exams at Key Stages 2, 4 and 5, they have become the end goal rather than a measure. You know how exams went for you: you revised, you did the test and then you forgot everything that you ever learnt in the subject. Sometimes the occasion was marked by throwing your books away or burning them on the garden barbecue!

Imagine instead an assessment which grades you on a project in which you have had to investigate a question that does not have a definitive answer. You have produced a report of your findings. The outcome of your work is the publication of your findings: perhaps as a written report, perhaps as a presentation. In the arts subjects, the assessment might well lead to the publication of a book or the exhibition of a piece of art. These more practical and meaningful assessments last so much longer in the memory. They also provide a good grounding for creative and thoughtful approaches to the needs of real-world challenges and change.

There is a generation of school leavers (and I mean the successful, not just the disaffected) who see through what they perceive as meaningless exams and hold them in very low regard. I think that it is much harder for children and teenagers to see the issues around high-stakes examinations. Adults are telling them that exams are important. Adults are also telling a good number of them that they are not meeting the standards expected. It is not only wrong to be passing such a negative judgement on a pupil with such a thin measure, it is also morally bankrupt to prepare our children for their adult lives in this way.

The young have stopped waiting for adults to get rid of exams (whilst the adults think they still need them to measure their schools by). They understand the limits of testing. A generation of young people, who watched as their teachers explicitly gamed the exams, know full well that the exams are/were no more than ill-fitting measurements of memory. The young don't really care about the outcomes of these tests. Ask them what they look for in a potential employee and you will hear about a 'people person', a 'friendly person' or a 'creative person'. You don't hear much about the need for a formal curriculum vitae or evidence of the grades that anyone has achieved.

Of course, the young will continue to play the game to an extent, knowing the importance of grades in university admissions criteria. They need the piece of paper to access the institution and, by default, certain professions. We need to invest in the education of those young people that will become leaders in their fields. A generation that is losing faith in its educational experience is adding a new problem for our higher education colleges and universities, alongside the fact that tuition fees have made university an option rather than what's expected of those who do well in exams.

I asked all of my interviewees if they went into higher education. University attendees formed a healthy majority; 70% had gone to university. I asked them why they had (or hadn't) gone. As a starting point, I borrowed a list of reasons for going to university from the 2017 International Student Survey.[2]

The options were:

1. Because I was passionate about the subject that I went on to study.

2. To continue my personal development and learning.

3. I needed the qualification for the particular career I want to pursue.

4. Intellectual challenge was an important factor.

5. So that I could learn essential life skills.

6. To help me get a job/a better job.

7. Because I wanted a change of direction in my life.

8. So that I would earn more money in the future having gained a degree.

9. For independence and freedom (to be my own person).

10. I saw university as a natural progression from school.

11. I wanted to experience university life and have a good time.

12. To meet new people from other places.

13. It was an opportunity to make a fresh start where no one knew me.

14. So that I had time to decide what to do with my life.

---

2 QS Enrolment Solutions, International Student Survey 2017: Welcoming the World – Maintaining the UK's Status as a Top Global Study Destination (2017), p. 10. Available at: https://www.internationalstudentsurvey.com/international-student-survey-2017/.

15. Because it was expected of me to go to university.

16. Everyone I knew was going to university and I didn't want to be left behind.

This list is comprised of the top 16 answers in a 60,000-student survey. The students were asked to give three reasons, and they are listed in order of frequency as a top-three answer. Being passionate about a subject was given as one of the three reasons by 58.4% of respondents; everyone was going and I didn't want to be left behind was given by 9.1%.

When I collated the answers that I received from my interviewees, I got responses as follows (with the chart position from the survey in brackets for comparison):

1. Because I was passionate about the subject that I went on to study. (1)

2. I needed the qualification for the particular career I want to pursue. (3)

3. To help me get a job/a better job. (6)

4. Because I wanted a change of direction in my life. (7)

5. To continue my personal development and learning. (2)

6. Intellectual challenge was an important factor. (4)

7. To meet new people from other places. (12)

8. Everyone I knew was going to university and I didn't want to be left behind. (16)

9. So that I could learn essential life skills. (5)

10. So that I would earn more money in the future having gained a degree. (8)

11. For independence and freedom (to be my own person). (9)

12. I saw university as a natural progression from school. (10)

13. I wanted to experience university life and have a good time. (11)

14. So that I had time to decide what to do with my life. (14)

15. Because it was expected of me to go to university. (15)

'It was an opportunity to make a fresh start where no one knew me' (13) was not mentioned at all.

I also asked those who did not go to university why they made that choice. Here are their answers, also in rank order:

1. I had had enough of education.

2. I decided to take a gap year and just never got around to going.

3. I started work.

4. I did not want to take on the debt of going to university.

5. It didn't interest me.

6. I didn't get the grades to go.

7. I wanted to get straight into work.

8. I took up an apprenticeship.

9. I couldn't afford to go.

The increase in the number of graduates, which I have already discussed, must have led to some devaluing of a university education: more people with degrees means they stand out less. But beyond this, I'd argue that university degrees are not viewed to have the same intrinsic value that they once did. In 2016, the international publishing company Penguin Random House removed having a degree as an essential requirement when seeking a job with them.[3] They want to make access more inclusive. They say that if people have talent and potential then they will be interested in an application from them.

------

3 Sean Coughlan, Penguin Scraps Degree Requirement, *BBC News* (18 January 2016). Available at: https://www.bbc.co.uk/news/education-35343680.

There is an increasing interest in what are sometimes called 'soft skills'. There is a genuine value in being personable, for example. The young really buy into this when choosing who to work with and what to invest in. In a sense, they are buying into the person as well as the product. Being able to adapt to different situations is another attribute that is increasingly valued. An ability to manage time is also important. Strong digital skills are no longer a bonus; they are an essential. The worker without those digital skills is soon going to be left behind.

With the current curriculum in place, students are no longer going to leave school – regardless of how good that schooling was – with a set of skills that will last them a lifetime. That is no longer a realistic goal. The exams that they are sitting now have such a limited lifespan, both in terms of the practical uses that the retained information can be put to in the real world and also in terms of that 'knowledge' quickly becoming out of date. We are only as wise as we are. Knowledge is only as wise as we are. What we understand keeps growing. Knowledge will grow with that expansion in capability. We mustn't see knowledge as static and immovable. I am sure that in a hundred years' time people will look back at us today and wonder why children used to be gathered together in school buildings every day and asked to remember stuff in their heads.

During the 2019 exam season, the BBC shared the heartwarming story of a 16-year-old boy from Stevenage who has cerebral palsy and who took his GCSEs using eye movement technology.[4] His mother is quoted as saying, 'He's now starting to look at his future career.' The obvious irony here is that it is not the GCSEs that are empowering this young man to contemplate his future, but the technology that will allow him a good level of articulacy in the adult world of work.

---

4   BBC News, Stevenage Pupil Taking GCSEs Using Eye Movement (15 May 2019). Available at: https://www.bbc.co.uk/news/av/uk-england-beds-bucks-herts-48269031/stevenage-pupil-taking-gcses-using-eye-movement.

In completing this chapter, I wanted to write a pen portrait for Ben, one of my interviewees. I looked at his Facebook page and found that he had done the job for me. After the GCSE exam results were released on 22 August 2019, Ben wrote the following advice to young people who were picking up theirs:

'For anyone who's not got their qualifications then don't worry. It's not the end of your path. I didn't get no grade higher than a 'C' in school (and that was in f-ing cooking). I went to college from leaving school and did a year at brickwork. Didn't stick it and went to work at Tesco. From there I worked in a factory aged 18 to 21 working night shifts, afternoons and mornings (I hated it) then from there I worked at another factory 21–23 (hated it). But now at 25 I'm 10 months away from becoming a qualified bricklayer. Last year I passed FINALLY my English and this year I've got my maths to do. Being 16 or whatever you might look into the future and think I NEED a job for life, I NEED a house, a mortgage. I NEED a nice car. I NEED to be on good £££. Because the government and the way things are get put across puts so much pressure on your shoulders ... but take it from someone with experience; if you have tunnel vision then well done but it took me a good few years to be focused and have my own tunnel vision for my path ... just do your thing and it'll work out in the end.'

At school, Ben had felt the pressure of predicted grades. The things that he needed at school that barred him from achieving were motivation and confidence. Without these ingredients, he gave up on literacy and numeracy during Year 9. He can now acknowledge that he got into trouble and fell behind because he was bored. He says that he used to make excuses for himself and settled for what he had, but now realises that honest hard graft can produce some of the changes that you want to see in your life. I think that Ben would tell you that he wishes that he'd listened more in school, fooled around a little less and understood that school might have been there for him, but his experience of school just didn't tell him these things.

Interestingly, Ben now wants to broaden his horizons, and so often travels abroad, largely to Europe. He buys a plane ticket and just goes. He chooses somewhere he hasn't been before. When he is there, wherever it is, he just makes friends. He strikes up conversations with the locals and manages to make enough contacts to get the inside view of the place. Ben lives in a fairly rural town in Derbyshire and wants to see more of the world, whilst also loving where he lives. Travelling is one of the ways in which Ben finds happiness in his life.

Ben told me that he'd like to use his bricklaying skills to help people. He has a vision of helping to build houses where they are needed most, perhaps in the third world. With his determination to prove that he can get qualified, and his independent spirit that takes him abroad, I am more than confident that Ben will achieve his ambitions.

Chapter 11
DISCRIMINATION

One area that I covered in the interviews was about the problems that young people had encountered and any discrimination that they felt they had suffered in their business lives. A good number felt that they had been discriminated against and there were numerous types of ill-treatment detailed.

Over the last few years austerity has bitten hard. The young have suffered in a number of ways. It has been difficult to arrange credit for business purposes and to have the confidence to invest in a business that might not take off.

When it comes to the notion of class, it is clear that there is no level playing field and that those living in poverty face an uphill struggle to lift themselves out of their predicament. The levels of income and investment that parents are able to support their children with have a rather obvious impact upon the speed with which those children can develop their business initiatives. The Bank of Mum and Dad can be a significant leg up, but not everyone is able to draw money there. Equally important is the message that you receive from parents and teachers about what it is going to be possible for you to do. When your mum and dad say you've got no chance, that prophecy tends to come true.

Regardless of economic background, the young were three and a half times more likely to be unemployed than older adults in the first quarter of 2014.[1] This situation has not got any better for our young workers over the subsequent years. Their chances of getting a mortgage are also very slim. It is no wonder that more and more of our young are turning to

1   Gould, *Wasted*, p. 90.

self-employment to make a living. Sometimes start-up businesses begin on the flimsiest of budget plans.

'People look at me sometimes and I can see them thinking "How's he managing to keep his business running?"'

In May 2018, American journalist Anna Bahney reported on statistics from the Federal Reserve Board which showed that 40% of Americans could not find US$400 if they had an unexpected emergency bill to pay.[2] I asked my interviewees a similar question about their personal finances and 55% said that they would struggle to cover that kind of bill instantly. Some said that they would have to sell something or get a loan. There is a general sense of fragility in the finances of the young. Those from economically disadvantaged family backgrounds are less likely to invest and less likely to save. They are less likely to have money for up-front payments for their business needs. They are more nervous about money altogether. Some would say that they lack aspiration, but this is palpably not true. What they lack is twofold: money to invest in their ideas, and opportunity.

Racial tension was prevalent in the work lives of some of my interviewees who are from minority ethnic backgrounds. It manifested itself in a range of ways, from overtly racist remarks and bullying to casual remarks that revealed the lack of equal opportunity that being non-white can present. It's truly horrifying to hear that this is still happening in this day and age. My young interviewees felt that they were part of a generally tolerant generation, although they recognised that the actions of the likes of Donald Trump and Nigel Farage had made it more acceptable to talk about migrants in racist terms, with the excuse of 'I'm only saying what everyone is

---

2   Anna Bahney, 40% of Americans Can't Cover a $400 Emergency Expense, *CNN Money* (22 May 2018). Available at: https://money.cnn.com/2018/05/22/pf/emergency-expenses-household-finances/index.html.

thinking.' Thankfully this is not what everyone is thinking and our young thoroughly reject Trump and his vile chants of 'Send them back.' The young have nothing but contempt in their hearts for such behaviour.

Gender bias was an issue that the men that I interviewed, on the whole, thought of as only being an issue for women. One female respondent told me that in her work as a wedding photographer she is often approached by middle-aged male guests who turn out to just 'want to out-tech me'. They like to tell her what she should be doing and how to operate her cameras. They also like to tell her what she is doing wrong! She is sure that they would not be so quick to approach a male professional photographer in the same way. Women working in male-dominated environments said they suffered sexual taunts and harassment offered as joking. The women who reported this kind of behaviour said that they had been called out for being too young, too weak and too girly.

Unfair practice around competition was an aspect of discrimination that worried my young interviewees more than most other forms. Whilst sexual harassment and derogatory comments were seen as clearly and immediately wrong, there was greyness to the area of competition. It felt more like part of being in business. However, there were some practices that clearly discriminated against young people. Older and more experienced people often take advantage of any hint of naivety about rules, procedures, laws or modes of conduct.

Most of the young people who felt that they'd been discriminated against told me that these incidents had come as a surprise and that they had not really been prepared to suffer in these ways. They have been paid late, underpaid and not paid at all. Some have been beaten up, threatened and spat on. They have been locked out, and locked in. They have been told that their work is too expensive and too cheap. They've been told that it's a man's game, no job for a woman and that they're getting it wrong. 'You don't know what you're doing.' They've been told that they are too young in any case. 'Get back to school. Get back to your mam. Does your mam know you're out? Don't mess with the big boys.'

The internet emboldens people to say things that they'd never say to a person's face. The screen can offer a certain detachment and a sense that what you write is not real. Making a racist, homophobic or sexist remark on the internet can be brushed aside with comments like 'I was only joking, where's your sense of humour?'

Youth is also a major cause of discrimination. There seems to be an inherent mistrust of the younger generation – those 'snowflake millennials' – and the economic odds are stacked against them too. When we look at the decline in real terms pay, the rise in interest rates, the denuding of pension pots and the impossibility of getting reasonable loans or a mortgage, how are the young meant to catch up? It is clear that the old are robbing the young of their adult life.

And still they rise …

Chapter 12

WHAT DO CHILDREN NEED TO KNOW IN FIFTEEN YEARS' TIME?

'From English I guess I have learnt to write and from maths I can add up pretty well … but I'm struggling to see what I have usefully learnt elsewhere, given that I spent so many years in school.'

I have visited this question before. It remains, however, as difficult to answer as ever. It is a question that changed how I felt about the curriculum and my own teaching of that curriculum entirely. I had spent years just handing out the curriculum that I was given without thinking about its usefulness. Now I am certain that the traditional curriculum will not do anymore, so we must return to the question of what we do with it. I think that this is an even more difficult question to answer as the future keeps lapping at the sandbags of our inertia. We need to stop blocking the flood and start thinking about how we move the curriculum and the school to higher ground – somewhere that will be productive for our future needs.

When you consider the curriculum that you offer, can you identify which parts of it may well be relevant in informing the lives of your students as they move into adulthood? In geography, for instance, it strikes me that I can see value in looking at climate change and the associated migrations of people that are precipitated by the earth's changing environments. Reviewing your curriculum, where is the value in what is being taught?

I think that there is a case to be made for project work around 'contemporary studies'. The subjects that might particularly feed into this would be history, geography, politics and citizenship – particularly around concern for the environment. When we look at the curriculum offers of these subjects, what can we recognise as being most relevant in each subject in supporting children to understand their world and prepare for involvement in the adult world? We need an overhaul of subject content – away from the sense of the curriculum being justified on its own merit to considering its utility in informing and inspiring our children.

This is one area in which children can be encouraged to explore important and engaging questions for themselves, such as:

- Why do wars happen?
- Why does the world keep getting warmer?
- What does it mean to be happy?
- Who, over the last 200 years, has been in my family?
- How can I be kind to the planet?
- How do you make a ...?
- I'd like to write a book. How do you do that?
- What does it mean to vote?
- How do I speak up about the issues I care about?

Chapter 13

WHAT CAN SCHOOLS DO RIGHT NOW TO AVOID BEING LEFT BEHIND?

Firstly, I'd like to say that I am evidently not claiming that this is rocket science. Secondly, this is not my list; it is a list of what school leavers are saying that they needed. These are the skills and attributes that they have needed in the early stages of their adult lives, in both a personal and a business capacity.

My interviewees explicitly told me that a good number of the things on this list were not available at school (or at least not evidently so, which amounts to the same thing). Can you check your school aims and ambitions and your hopes for the curriculum to see how you are measuring up and how you might move towards providing an education that addresses these needs?

Explicitly teach confidence

This is challenging because confidence is a feeling that you can't just tell children they should have. There are, however, a number of ways in which we can address the topic of confidence and its importance.

- Begin to discuss and promote confidence with the children.

- Write opportunities to demonstrate confidence into the curriculum in each subject and into the wider activities of the school.

- According to my interviewees, confidence means believing that you have something to say and that you are articulate enough to say it. One of the positive things that school was praised for by some of my interviewees was the opportunity to speak in front of groups of people, both adults and peers. Of course, in the English curriculum, children are no longer graded on that aspect of communication. This has weakened its importance in the eyes of both overworked teachers and children who have been told/taught to follow the marks.

- In Chapter 8 we saw a list of the characteristics of creative people. One of these aspects is preferring to 'work independently'. However, most of my interviewees understood the collaborative nature of business and the need to develop projects with others. Schools are making use of group work, sometimes with individual responsibilities within groups. This is something that is reflected in the adult world of work. Collaborating effectively will support growing confidence.

- To make school projects authentic, they should result in a meaningful outcome. I think that projects should be long-term initiatives with concrete outcomes. The 'get into a group for a lesson, write ideas on a piece of A3 paper and then throw it in the bin at the end' type of work is limited. A project tackled over a number of weeks – with deadlines and a genuine purpose – will last longer in the memory and provide a better model of how to work collaboratively.

Teach digital proficiency

Having good knowledge about the various means of communicating, and how they work, is also an essential skill. By this I mean both the mechanics of manipulating websites and social media and also how and when to best employ communications. Big data knows how to control the internet; your students could use some tuition regarding this. Your pupils also need a critical eye and a dose of healthy scepticism. You shouldn't just receive meaning; you should make it. Supporting children to be discerning in what they consider to be true and of value is really important.

- Acknowledge the way in which society really communicates. Try to look past exercise books and pens. Look to offer opportunities to present work in digital formats as the norm.

- Train young people in the productive use of the internet. There is a dangerous presumption that they can all 'do it', but many of our young will need support in using technology meaningfully.

- Write the use of digital resources into the curriculum, including making use of ICT in innovative ways to create and present work. Look for audiences for pupils' work. The digital audience is huge.

- Develop online portfolios in which pupils can collect their work, a record of what they've read and a record of their experiences and skills.

- Promote an ability to make use of, and maintain a healthy scepticism towards, social media and the associated algorithms.

- Look to increase the amount of personalised learning that is undertaken by pupils. Look to adapt the curriculum so that pupils can work with study tools that are adapted to their individual needs. This will help develop a self-paced curriculum. Instigate frequent skills tests that support incremental gains as study progresses.

- Look to increase the implementation of e-learning platforms. There is going to be a significant shift towards online platforms, which will include VR, AR and multi-perspective platforms. E-learning is proving to be affordable and it is making the study–life balance much more manageable.

- I am confident that the use of games and apps for learning will increase and that this will lead to more creative and practical approaches in the curriculum. Students are going to be assessed on critical thinking and problem-solving skills in the coming years. These are the skills that are going to be increasingly sought-after in the world of work. Examinations are going to be replaced with creative projects which will be evidenced in e-portfolios and cloud spaces. We all need to prepare for this advance.

- We need to think about the real ways in which we communicate and sort out the English and ICT curriculum offers. There are so many ways in which the English curriculum is out of date and fails to support children to become effective communicators. The fightback against the internet is futile: it is the communication medium of our age. Writing with paper and a pen is also anachronistic. The adult world does not work this way. We must help children investigate how to write in the ways that they will actually need in future.

- Voice and tone (considering the appropriateness for the audience, purpose and context) remain at the heart of the matter. However, for exam boards to continue to mistrust the internet as being without specified audience is, again, futile. Children need to be able to write appropriately in digital formats and have the capacity to navigate and read materials online. We can support them to think about the make-up of potential and target audiences.

Teach money management

This was a strong theme in the interviews. Children are leaving school with very little understanding of how to manage money. An appreciation of interest rates, hire purchase and rent/mortgage rates will be increasingly important as more of us have less.

- Create space in the timetable to teach about budgeting and debt.
- The end of physical money is upon us. Spending will only be a click away everywhere. How will you teach value moving forward? How will you teach moderation and forward planning?

Promote strategies for well-being

A passive education of waiting to be told what to write, think and know featured highly in the interviews as a real turn-off and something that disadvantaged the young when they wanted to get up and running as adults. Such passivity fails to inculcate hard work and enterprise. It also helps to create a person whose instinct is to wait to be told what to think and do. This is a really low aspiration for our pupils. We can aim higher and offer them a much stronger vision of their own agency. Here are a few ideas for starters:

- Present well-being as a choice.
- Teach time management, including work–life balance.
- Consider online safety and conduct.
- Explicitly teach about healthy choices regarding relationships, diet and exercise.

Make sure that young people leave school fully prepared for the world of work

Our young people need to develop 21st-century skills that will give them a strong chance of being employable or finding a self-employed niche.

In considering how business is moving forward, the World Economic Forum predicted that the top skills that would be required in 2020 are as follows:[1]

- Critical thinking requires that you are able to understand the way in which ideas are linked together. You will need to be able to determine the importance and relevance of arguments and then build on these arguments. Taking a systematic approach and spotting mistakes are important to the success of critical thinking. You would also need the capacity to reflect on how your own assumptions, beliefs and values might impact on your perspective. Solving complex problems requires a good working memory and an ability to think in flexible ways to come up with solutions.

- Cognitive flexibility is the ability to change the way in which you look at something and an ability to appreciate that others may have a different perspective. It is also the ability to step away from your usual way of thinking and adapt and move on due to a new set of circumstances. This is what I have referred to as the ability to learn, unlearn and relearn. The faster change happens, the more this capacity is going to be important. Businesses rely on judgement and decision-making.

---

1   Alex Gray, The 10 Skills You Need to Thrive in the Fourth Industrial Revolution, *World Economic Forum* (19 January 2016). Available at: https://www.weforum.org/agenda/2016/01/the-10-skills-you-need-to-thrive-in-the-fourth-industrial-revolution/.

- Creativity is a skill that relies on the capacity to develop beyond what is known and into the realms of imagination.

- There are also those skills that centre around working with clients and co-workers. The ability to manage people – whether that is coordinating with other people or building a common understanding through negotiation – is important in providing a service orientation.

- Emotional intelligence is important in understanding how others feel and, indeed, in being able to reflect on how you feel.

These are the skills that businesses recognise that they need and are hoping to develop. They are also the skills that the self-employed will need in order to prosper. Where are they in your curriculum? When are these skills discussed explicitly with the pupils? It might well be that you are already delivering on a good deal of this. I think we need to make the pupils aware that they are learning these skills and they also need to understand the importance of developing strength in these areas.

Furthermore, we need to review our attitude towards mistake-making. My interviewees report making many, many mistakes. Their general stance has been that mistakes are necessary and that you need to learn from them and not get too down about not being right first time, every time. Can we support pupils to know that it is okay – that it's completely normal – to make mistakes? Can we help them to appreciate the value of a mistake?

Promote opportunities for independent thinking and collaborative projects

This needs to happen in all corners of the curriculum, across all subjects. The ability to work through a project from start to finish – dealing with all aspects of concept design to finished product (whatever that product might be) – and having the chance to discuss and plan with others are vital aspects of contemporary learning. Not only do these experiences provide vital tools for learning, they are the actual ways in which our young people are developing their own learning in adult life.

Reinstate the school trip immediately

It lasts long in the memory. There is evidence that those working in natural environments and/or outside the classroom do better in core subjects such as English and maths. Engaging environments promote deep, long-term memories.[2]

Rethink the role of the teacher

In the coming years the idea of the teacher as a guide to learning will gain power. The expert skill of the teacher will develop from the passing on of information – 'knowledge', if you will – to supporting pupils to work out where their strengths, interests and values lie. One main function here

---

2 King's College London, Understanding the Diverse Benefits of Learning in Natural Environments [research paper] (April 2011). Available at: http://www. lotc.org.uk/wp-content/uploads/2011/09/KCL-LINE-benefits-final-version.pdf.

will be to support pupils in an investigative approach to learning (see Chapter 3).

Make social and emotional skills a priority

Promoting the idea of emotional intelligence and sociability as skills is important. If our young people are to prosper in their work lives, they must develop a whole range of communication skills, such as being able to present themselves and their ideas, and being able to collaborate in networking situations.

Can we help our pupils to define and explore how they feel about things? In the post-truth era, this has become vital. Opportunities for children to voice their feelings and to listen to the thoughts of others will increase their sense of self-worth. A number of interviewees reported having left school being 'naive' and without having really thought about, or formed, opinions of their own. Outsourcing thinking to search engines will lead to a fairly thoughtless and dependent population.

Abolish uniform

Not one of my interviewees had any use or time for school uniform. It is a concept that they wholly reject. This is a reflection of the ways in which the world of work is moving away from uniform decisions (excuse the pun!) about clothing. The message of uniformity flies in the face of how the young want to express their own personalities.

The domains of formality in our society are shrinking in a number of ways. The way in which we speak to each other and the ways in which we dress at work are becoming more informal. There needs to be an understanding in schools that uniform is an ephemeral aspect of education. It is merely an organising aspect of a school, not a function. I didn't receive any positive comments about having to wear a uniform. It was largely regarded as one of the means of controlling children. The idea that it was important in teaching them that you had to 'dress up' for work was entirely rejected.

Support staff in recognising change and its impact on their practice

Delivering strong continuing professional development (CPD) that acknowledges that the curriculum needs to change to meet the ways in which our society is developing is hugely important. Our teachers will feel more confident when they can see the value of what they are being asked to deliver. A number of key skills need to be broached in terms of staff training: teaching confidence, digital proficiency, etc. For instance, 'literacy' is conveyed in how teachers use language as well as how children are explicitly taught to develop their capacities. It needs to be embedded as practice across the curriculum and in the norms of the classroom.

In my experience, roughly a third of staff will be interested in developing their own competencies through school initiatives. They will join working parties, reading groups, etc. The remainder can be resistant to change/'newness'. ('I already do that! I don't need to think about how I teach.') Reflect on how you could support staff:

- Who are the key staff who will support the developments that you want to foster?
- How will you involve all staff? (For example, might you write a book together?)

- How will you make sure that any initiative around literacy/articulacy does not just become the responsibility of a coordinator?

- Do you want to plan a curriculum for developing your pupils' presence of mind?

Children are offered a diet of knowledge retention, remembering facts that go largely unexplained in terms of why they are being learnt or what their use will be. The model is passive non-participatory reception, presenting old knowledge to be remembered and then demonstrated in a test of memory. This will have been the norm for most teachers throughout their careers. Many new teachers have yet to experience anything else.

- Can we support our teachers to adapt and develop their understanding of teaching?

- Do we understand the ways in which the learning 'ecosystem' is changing?

- How do our lesson structures and default approaches suit the ways in which children increasingly like to learn?

- Can we adapt schemes of work to include 'new knowledge' approaches?

Pay particular attention to the importance of literacy and oracy

People with larger vocabularies tend to be intrigued by words.

Isabel L. Beck, Margaret G. McKeown and Linda Kucan[3]

Since 2013, children have been in receipt of explicit language training in Years 5 and 6. Their schools are being rated, in part, on the results of spelling, punctuation and grammar (SPaG) tests. This is a high-stakes part of the curriculum for primary schools and they will have prepared their students thoroughly for these tests. Focusing on tests distracts from what's really important: developing children's capacities to communicate. Not only that, but the kind of literacy that it is testing is very close to becoming obsolete, in the way in which gramophones have. There are better and new ways to measure literacy and to support its development. What it means to be literate is changing due to developments in the ways in which we communicate, largely through digital mediums.

We need to train our teachers so that they are competent and feel confident in supporting articulacy in children. This means being informed about what communication mediums people are using (in business and in their personal lives) and how these mediums work. There is much work to be done here. Furthermore, are our teachers able to make good the connection between knowing things (declarative knowledge) and supporting the children in articulating and applying that knowledge (procedural knowledge)? Making sure that our

---

3 Isabel L. Beck, Margaret G. McKeown and Linda Kucan, *Bringing Words to Life: Robust Vocabulary Instruction*, 2nd edn (New York: The Guilford Press, 2013), p. 13.

children 'know' things is no longer the primary function of teaching in the 21st century.

Rethink how we track progress

Can you give some detailed thought to the way in which you track the progress of each individual pupil in terms of their experience of the curriculum and their aptitude? This is not about collecting data about expectations of how they'll perform in terminal exams. This is about keeping an online record of what has been experienced in school and the growing understanding and competence that has been demonstrated. Included would be examples of projects and their most successful pieces of work. It would be a store of the reading that the pupil has undertaken. It would be cloud-based and follow that child through their school life, remaining available for them to access in adulthood.

I believe that we need to give thought to what is basic and required of all, and what are the advanced aspects of the curriculum which should be opted into. The national curriculum in England, for example, dictates that everyone must do some form of English and maths at school. The curriculum is set and fixed, outlining the base of skills deemed necessary. Science of some sort is also a requirement at GCSE. The rationale that we need scientists and engineers is often offered. In some schools, a modern foreign language (MFL) is also mandatory in Key Stage 4. The advent of in-ear real-time translators and language apps on phones will increasingly challenge young people's desire to learn a foreign language.

Could we have a curriculum that is navigated by options that genuinely track a child's interests and competencies? On the back of that, could we create an assessment structure that documents the real progress made, rather than ascribing numbers to notional levels of acumen? By this I mean a personal portfolio that details what has been experienced, what has been produced and the quality of the outcomes: a genuine space and purpose for reporting what has been achieved and the potential that lies ahead.

Whilst we are considering how we track progress, do we need to rethink age-related expectations and how we use this to organise learning? The use of grouping children by age is proving to be what Nicholas Negroponte describes as a 'useless myth … for ease of convenience'.[4] Do younger and older people work together in the adult world? Ah … yes, they do!

Think about what you want your pupils to do in school

What do you think that all children should have the opportunity to do before they leave school? Here are some examples, taken from a list of 100 compiled by the *TES*. Think about the real-world capacities that we'd be building if this were explicitly written into the ways in which we use our time in schools:

Make good friends. Get covered in paint/mud/chalk. Take part in a school production. Go swimming. Take part in a sports tournament. Go on a school trip. Get a certificate. Experience other schools. Learn how to get on with everyone. Invent something. Make a fool out of yourself/embarrass yourself. Work with children from older year groups. Grow some flowers or vegetables. Learn to feel confident in front of the class. Be a leader of a group. Raise money for charity. Run a stall at the fair. Teach part of a lesson to your class. Make a best friend. Take part in outdoor learning. Ride a bike and take cycling proficiency. Be in the local newspaper. Fail so that you can improve from your mistake. Feel

4 In his foreword to Sugata Mitra's *Beyond the Hole in the Wall*, loc. 40.

happy and safe. Go to an after-school club. Find out that you are good at something. Find out about different cultures. Be caring. Discover your favourite author. Take part in a special event. Hatch chicks in an incubator. Read a book on the grass on a sunny day. Be kind to someone who needs a friend. Listen to a ghost story. Go pond dipping. Dress up for World Book Day. Try different types of food. Learn basic first aid and how to dial 999. Film and edit a movie. Have a pen pal. Help younger pupils at school. Have your parents come to visit the school. Learn to look after yourself.[5]

If children leave your school having experienced all of these things, then they will have made a great start on the road to real-world proficiency.

The way in which children come to a physical school building, sit passively in receipt of old knowledge and then get measured by what they can remember will be swept away for two simple reasons: firstly, it doesn't serve the needs of society and, secondly, the young have lost respect for it. Reflecting on the questions that I have posed in this chapter will mean that you are a bit more prepared for the shifts coming in education than you would be if you keep repeating the formula of today. Please don't wait for change to come from government; they are off somewhere else. Don't wait for the exam boards to usher in change; they are too invested in selling revision guides. Change will come because our young stop paying attention to what is not worth listening to anymore.

5 *TES* Reporter, 100 Things You Should Have Done at School Before the Age of 11 – Chosen by Primary Pupils, *TES* (22 July 2016). Available at: https://www.tes.com/news/100-things-you-should-have-done-school-age-11-chosen-primary-pupils. *TES* – the online and weekly education magazine for teachers (www.tes.com/news).

Chapter 14
'FINAL DECISIONS ARE MADE IN SILENT ROOMS'[1]

Our young people are telling us that they do not like the world that we are offering them; they are going to collaborate to take the world that they inherit off in a different direction. They want some of the things that we have decided they cannot have anymore, like home ownership and a thoughtful education. Owning a home is a distant dream and formal schooling is so see-through that it is far more productive to find out how to do the things you want to do on YouTube. They also don't want some of the things that we have decided they can have – like Brexit and centralised, big-business, capitalist-driven 'culture'. Our young want the place where they live to be local and supportive. They are for local ethical businesses and for the opportunity to engage, collaborate and switch professions often in their lives. They also want to travel and they want their chosen destinations to be different to home. Because they mainly speak amongst themselves about all of this, they are losing respect for the concept of authority. You don't speak to your jailer about how to escape. It's a matter of trust, and that trust is going fast.

So our schools need to respond to a new society built on diversity, ethical decisions and care of the planet. We must reinvent our curriculum so that it more closely mirrors the world around our children. They spend too much time at school sat down and in receipt of convergent thinking. The adult lives they will lead require some deeper independent

---

1 The title of this chapter is taken from Carl Sandburg's poem 'A Father Sees a Son Nearing Manhood'.

thought. Instead of promoting a curriculum that is being trimmed to offer children a culturally thin idea of British values, perhaps we should be pursuing questions such as, 'Why is my curriculum white?' Finding out the answers to that question is a project worth engaging with I'd say.

We can no longer deny the impact of the internet. It has many positive features and raises a good deal of issues that need our urgent attention. But it is pervasive; it is how the young communicate and how they receive most of their information about life. Refusing to involve ourselves with its existence just will not do. That is negligence.

What were once deemed 'soft' skills are actually the tools of survival in these uncertain times. Confidence, creativity, divergent thinking, the ability to communicate, healthy scepticism and digital proficiency: explicit teaching around these key skills is essential.

Piggy Lambert, head coach of Purdue University basketball team, reflected:

The team that makes most mistakes usually wins.[2]

The sense that life involves trial and error and that you will make mistakes – and that the best thing to do is learn from those mistakes – is not a message currently prevalent in our school system. This has to change if the pupils of today are to become the well-adjusted adults of the future. The young people who I interviewed told me many times over about the challenge of looking at their mistakes and trying to make sense of them to assess how they might proceed. This is no light thing. We need to support creative and resourceful thinking about life's hurdles. Otherwise, in this age of loneliness, the young can quickly sink. Our exam-driven 'curriculum'

---

2 Quoted in Seth Davis, *Wooden: A Coach's Life* (New York: Times Books, 2014), p. 156.

leads children from A to B by the shortest route, requiring the 'right answer' first time, every time. It's no preparation for life. Furthermore, young people have all kinds of energies that are not required or assessed in schools. We need to promote a broader definition of what success might mean. The narrow confines of the assessment of academic intelligence in a high-stakes examination is in no way useful in determining the full merits and abilities of our young.

It falls to the older generations to look after and nurture the generation that is coming of age next. The world is a difficult place. The certainty of what children need to be prepared for in their adult lives is no longer there. Our teachers have to make decisions about the education that will benefit their pupils. Can we support them to develop an immediate ability to face the future and a longer term desire to learn throughout their lives?

Every teacher must take control of their own classroom and make sure that the curriculum on offer is suitable for the children in front of them. Where that curriculum needs bending towards the needs and experiences of the children, it is the job of every teacher to make the curriculum fit. Outside of the classroom, teachers must speak up when the curriculum is of little use.

Teachers have an unmanageable job really. Teachers are time-poor, strapped for resources and forced to peddle a largely out-of-date and often dry curriculum. Yet our teachers remain vital: we need to trust them and be grateful for their determination to help the young. We need to support them with a relevant curriculum and the training necessary for them to keep pace with the developments that will affect their pupils' lives. Teachers are people with big hearts; we need to invest in that. In education presently, we have a tension between restrictive and limited policymaking and the genuine complexity of what an education should be. The sooner we all acknowledge that complexity – and stop trying to streamline education into a set of pre-packaged exam-focused units – the better. Let the teachers teach; they are the ones who know the children in front of them.

Similarly, the young people whose collective and individual voices appear in these pages are alive with potential. Forget notions of snowflakes and millennials burning up. Given half a chance and a bit of agency our young people want to make the very best of their opportunities with energy, passion and hard work. Hopefully I have helped them to express themselves and tell the rest of us what will be needed as part of a helpful, warm and relevant education for the 21st century. Listening to their voices has helped me to see ways in which we can support our young people in the years ahead. We all need to think about the education that we offer.

> 'People will tell you that you can't do it – that you're mad for trying – but you mustn't listen. It's about love ... if you love what you do, you'll find a way.'

Support them we must ...

AN AFTERTHOUGHT

In Series 5, Episode 2 of *Game of Thrones*, brave little Arya Stark arrives at the House of Black and White. She knocks on the door and pleads to be let in. She is denied access. As the enigmatic doorkeeper is closing the door, Arya cries, 'I have nowhere else to go!'

The doorkeeper simply replies, 'You have everywhere else to go.'

When you know that the curriculum is not serving the pupils in front of you and you can't see a way forward, always remember that you have everywhere else to go. There is another way.

REFERENCES AND READING LIST

References

Alini, Erica (2018). Apple Hits $1 Trillion in Value. Only 16 Countries Are Worth More, Global News (2 August). Available at: https://globalnews.ca/news/4367056/apple-1-trillion-market-cap/.

Bahney, Anna (2018). 40% of Americans Can't Cover a $400 Emergency Expense, *CNN Money* (22 May). Available at: https://money.cnn.com/2018/05/22/pf/emergency-expenses-household-finances/index.html.

Baker, Toby and Laurie Smith (2018). The Beginning of the End of Exams, *Nesta* (3 December). Available at: https://www.nesta.org.uk/feature/ten-predictions-2019/beginning-end-exams/.

BBC News (2019). Stevenage Pupil Taking GCSEs Using Eye Movement (15 May). Available at: https://www.bbc.co.uk/news/av/uk-england-beds-bucks-herts-48269031/stevenage-pupil-taking-gcses-using-eye-movement.

Beck, Isabel L., Margaret G. McKeown and Linda Kucan (2013). *Bringing Words to Life: Robust Vocabulary Instruction*, 2nd edn (New York: The Guilford Press).

Benn, Melissa (2018). *Life Lessons: The Case for a National Education Service* (London: Verso).

Bolton, Paul (2012). *Education: Historical Statistics*. Ref: SN/SG/4252, House of Commons Library (27 November).

Bonderud, Douglas (2019). Artificial Intelligence, Authentic Impact: How Educational AI Is Making the Grade, *Ed Tech* (12 August). Available at: https://edtechmagazine.com/k12/article/2019/08/artificial-intelligence-authentic-impact-how-educational-ai-making-grade-perfcon.

Brown-Martin, Graham (2018). Education and the Fourth Industrial Revolution, *Learning {Re}Imagined* (14 January). Available at: https://medium.com/learning-re-imagined/education-and-the-fourth-industrial-revolution-cd6bcd7256a3.

Burek, Owen (2019). 15 Vital Money Lessons You Should Have Been Taught in School, *Save the Student* (10 October). Available at: https://www.savethestudent.org/money/15-money-lessons.html.

Burke, Liz (2016). University Degrees 'Irrelevant' to Big Employers, *news.com.au* (29 January). Available at: https://www.news.com.au/finance/work/careers/university-degrees-irrelevant-to-big-employers/news-story/8a0340dd2b8c70c35b8ce3302c8d0cc5.

Carter, Caron (2016). Is Friendship Something That Can Be Taught in Schools?, *Sheffield Hallam University* [blog] (31 October). Available at: https://blogs.shu.ac.uk/sioe/2016/10/31/is-friendship-something-that-can-be-taught-in-schools-3/?doing_wp_cron=1564356381.8568780422210693359375.

Chapman, Ben (2019). HSBC to Introduce 40% Overdraft Interest Rate, Quadrupling Costs for Some Customers, *The Independent* (5 December). Available at: https://www.independent.co.uk/news/business/news/hsbc-overdraft-fees-interest-rate-rise-charges-christmas-spending-a9233821.html.

Collinson, Patrick (2019). Lloyds Unveils 100% Mortgage for First-Time Buyers, *The Guardian* (28 January). Available at: https://www.theguardian.com/money/2019/jan/28/lloyds-unveils-100-mortgage-for-first-time-buyers.

Coughlan, Sean (2016). Penguin Scraps Degree Requirement, *BBC News* (18 January). Available at: https://www.bbc.co.uk/news/education-35343680.

Daltrey, Roger (2018). *My Story: Thanks a Lot Mr Kibblewhite* (London: Blink Publishing).

Davis, Seth (2014). *Wooden: A Coach's Life* (New York: Times Books).

Dawkins, Richard, Daniel C. Dennett, Sam Harris and Christopher Hitchens (2019). *The Four Horsemen: The Discussion that Sparked an Atheist Revolution* (London: Bantam Press).

Dolan, Paul (2014). *Happiness by Design: Finding Pleasure and Purpose in Everyday Life* (London: Penguin).

Escueta, Maya, Vincent Quan, Andre Joshua Nickow and Philip Oreopoulos (2017). *Education Technology: An Evidence-Based Review*, NBER Working Paper No. 23744 (August). Available at: https://www.povertyactionlab.org/sites/default/files/publications/NBER-23744-EdTech-Review.pdf.

Fenwick, Victoria (2019). Are We Creating a Generation of Forrest Gumps?, *TES* (2 August). Available at: https://www.tes.com/news/are-we-creating-generation-forrest-gumps.

Gil, Natalie (2014). Loneliness: A Silent Plague That Is Hurting Young People Most, *The Guardian* (20 July). Available at: https://www.theguardian.com/lifeandstyle/2014/jul/20/loneliness-britains-silent-plague-hurts-young-people-most.

Gilbert, Ian (2011). *Why Do I Need a Teacher When I've Got Google?* (Abingdon: Routledge).

Glassdoor (2018). 15 More Companies That No Longer Require a Degree – Apply Now (14 August). Available at: https://blog-content.glassdoor.com/site-us/no-degree-required/.

Gould, Georgia (2016). *Wasted: How Misunderstanding Young Britain Threatens Our Future* (London: Abacus).

Gray, Alex (2016). The 10 Skills You Need to Thrive in the Fourth Industrial Revolution, *World Economic Forum* (19 January). Available at: https://www.weforum.org/agenda/2016/01/the-10-skills-you-need-to-thrive-in-the-fourth-industrial-revolution/.

Grice, Andrew (2012). 'Unlock the Closed-Shop Professions', *The Independent* (31 May). Available at: https://www.independent.co.uk/news/uk/politics/unlock-the-closed-shop-professions-7804981.html.

Hallahan, Grainne (2018). Why It's Time to Say Goodbye to Group Work, *TES* (10 March). Available at: https://www.tes.com/news/why-its-time-say-goodbye-group-work.

Hancox, Dan (2018). The Unstoppable Rise of Veganism: How a Fringe Movement Went Mainstream, *The Guardian* (1 April). Available at: https://www.theguardian.com/lifeandstyle/2018/apr/01/vegans-are-coming-millennials-health-climate-change-animal-welfare.

Harari, Yuval Noah (2018). *21 Lessons for the 21st Century* (London: Jonathan Cape).

King's College London (2011). Understanding the Diverse Benefits of Learning in Natural Environments [research paper] (April). Available at: http://www.lotc.org.uk/wp-content/uploads/2011/09/KCL-LINE-benefits-final-version.pdf.

Kiyosaki, Robert T. (2001). *The Business School for People Who Like Helping People* (Scottsdale, AZ: Cashflow Technologies Inc).

Knox, Patrick (2019). Youth Climate March: Thousands of Student Climate Change Protesters Descend on Central London in Record-Breaking Turnout, *The Sun* (24 May). Available at: https://www.thesun.co.uk/news/9145737/fridays-for-future-climate-change-protesters-110-countries/.

Kostelanetz, Richard (2003). *Conversing with Cage*, 2nd edn (New York and London: Routledge).

Lovelock, James (2019). *Novacene: The Coming Age of Hyperintelligence* (London: Allen Lane).

McDonnell, Adam and Chris Curtis (2019). How Britain Voted in the 2019 General Election, *YouGov* (17 December). Available at: https://yougov.co.uk/topics/politics/articles-reports/2019/12/17/how-britain-voted-2019-general-election.

Meltzer, Milton (2000 [1978]). *Dorothea Lange: A Photographer's Life* (Syracuse, NY: Syracuse University Press).

Mercadante, Kevin (2019). The Future of Cash – Will It Disappear or Become Obsolete?, *Money Under 30* (22 May). Available at: https://www.moneyunder30.com/what-is-the-future-of-cash.

Mitra, Sugata (2012). *Beyond the Hole in the Wall* [Kindle edition] (TED Books).

Mitra, Sugata (2014). The Future of Schooling: Children and Learning at the Edge of Chaos, *Prospects*, 44(4): 547–558.

Mlodinow, Leonard (2018). *Elastic: The Power of Flexible Thinking* (London: Penguin).

Monbiot, George (2014). The Age of Loneliness Is Killing Us, *The Guardian* (14 October). Available at: https://www.theguardian.com/commentisfree/2014/oct/14/age-of-loneliness-killing-us.

NAHT (2017). Schools Are 'Narrowing' the Curriculum, Says Ofsted (30 November). Available at: https://www.naht.org.uk/news-and-opinion/news/curriculum-and-assessment-news/schools-are-narrowing-the-curriculum-says-ofsted/.

National Debtline and Money Advice Trust (2016). *Borrowed Years: A Spotlight Briefing on Young People, Credit and Debt* (August). Available at: http://www.moneyadvicetrust.org/SiteCollection Documents/Research%20and%20reports/Borrowed%20Years%2c%20Young%20people%20credit%20and%20debt%2c%20Aug%202016.pdf.

Office for National Statistics (2019). Employment in the UK: December 2019 [statistical bulletin] (17 December). Available at: https://www.ons.gov.uk/employmentandlabourmarket/peopleinwork/employmentandemployeetypes/bulletins/employmentintheuk/december2019.

QS Enrolment Solutions (2017). International Student Survey 2017: Welcoming the World – Maintaining the UK's Status as a Top Global Study Destination. Available at: https://www.internationalstudentsurvey.com/international-student-survey-2017/.

Reilly, Katie (2019). Read Attorney General William Barr's Full Remarks Ahead of the Mueller Report Release, *Time* (18 April).

Available at: https://time.com/5573085/attorney-general-william-barr-transcript-mueller-report/.

Roseneil, Sasha and Shelley Budgeon (2014). Cultures of Intimacy and Care Beyond 'the Family': Personal Life and Social Change in the Early 21st Century, *Current Sociology*, 52(2): 135–159. Available at: https://www.researchgate.net/publication/249680246_Cultures_of_Intimacy_and_Care_Beyond_the_Family_Personal_Life_and_Social_Change_in_the_Early_21st_Century.

Snelson, Jacob (2017). The Digital Necessity, *Medium* (4 August). Available at: https://medium.com/digital-society/the-necessity-of-technology-85462f953910.

Staufenberg, Jess (2019). Computing Education in 'Steep Decline' after Reforms, Warns Report, *Schools Week* (8 May). Available at: https://schoolsweek.co.uk/computing-education-in-steep-decline-following-government-reforms-warns-new-report/.

Study International (2019). How Can Schools Prepare Students for the Fourth Industrial Revolution? (31 May). Available at: https://www.studyinternational.com/news/how-can-schools-prepare-students-for-the-fourth-industrial-revolution/.

Susskind, Jamie (2018). *Future Politics: Living Together in a World Transformed by Tech* (Oxford: Oxford University Press).

Susskind, Richard and Daniel Susskind (2015). *The Future of the Professions: How Technology Will Transform the Work of Human Experts* (Oxford: Oxford University Press).

Sutherland, John (2016). *The War on the Old* (London: Biteback Publishing).

Sutherland, John (2018). *The War on the Young* (London: Biteback Publishing).

TES Reporter (2016). 100 Things You Should Have Done at School Before the Age of 11 – Chosen by Primary Pupils, *TES* (22 July). Available at: https://www.tes.com/news/100-things-you-should-have-done-school-age-11-chosen-primary-pupils.

The Blue Swan Daily (2019). Targeting UK Millennials? New Insight Shows They Will Take and Spend More on Leisure Trips During 2019 in Spite of the Clouds Over Brexit (20 March). Available at: https://blueswandaily.com/targeting-uk-millennials-new-insight-shows-they-will-take-and-spend-more-on-leisure-trips-during-2019-in-spite-of-the-clouds-over-brexit/.

The Real News Network (2019). Sanders & Warren Pitch Rival Plans to Address $1.6 Trillion in Student Debt (27 June). Available at: https://therealnews.com/stories/sanders-warren-pitch-rival-plans-to-address-1-6-trillion-in-student-debt.

UCAS (2017). Largest Ever Proportion of UK's 18 Year Olds Entered Higher Education in 2017, UCAS Data Reveals (27 November). Available at: https://www.ucas.com/corporate/news-and-key-documents/news/largest-ever-proportion-uks-18-year-olds-entered-higher-education-2017-ucas-data-reveals.

Walker, Peter (2019). David Attenborough: Polluting Planet May Become as Reviled as Slavery, *The Guardian* (9 July). Available at: https://www.theguardian.com/tv-and-radio/2019/jul/09/david-attenborough-young-people-give-me-hope-on-environment.

Wardrop, Murray (2008). Learning by Heart Is 'Pointless for Google Generation', *The Telegraph* (2 December). Available at: https://www.telegraph.co.uk/education/primaryeducation/3540852/Learning-by-heart-is-pointless-for-Google-generation.html.

World Economic Forum (2016). *Future of Jobs Report: Employment, Skills and Workforce Strategy for the Fourth Industrial Revolution* (January). Available at: http://www3.weforum.org/docs/WEF_Future_of_Jobs.pdf.

A reading list

The books listed here are the ones that I have read in informing myself about the ways in which the world is moving on. Collectively they have allowed me to explain and explore the issues that were raised in the interviews.

Avent, Ryan (2017). *The Wealth of Humans: Work and Its Absence in the Twenty-First Century* (London: Penguin).

Bartlett, Jamie (2018). *The People Vs Tech: How the Internet Is Killing Democracy (and How We Save It)* (London: Ebury Press).

Bridle, James (2018). *New Dark Age: Technology and the End of the Future* (New York: Verso).

Brockman, John (2015). *What to Think About Machines That Think* (New York: Harper Perennial).

Carey, Benedict (2015). *How We Learn: Throw Out the Rule Book and Unlock Your Brain's Potential* (London: Pan Books).

Chakrabarti, Shami (2015). *On Liberty* (London: Penguin).

Chatfield, Tom (2012). *How to Thrive in the Digital Age* (London: Macmillan).

Claxton, Guy (2008). *What's the Point of School? Rediscovering the Heart of Education* (Oxford: Oneworld Publications).

Clegg, Nick (2017). *How to Stop Brexit (and Make Britain Great Again)* (London: The Bodley Head).

D'Ancona, Matthew (2017). *Post Truth: The New War on Truth and How to Fight Back* (London: Ebury Press).

Frase, Peter (2016). *Four Futures: Life After Capitalism* (London: Verso).

Gerritzen, Mieke and Koert van Mensvoort (2015). *Save the Humans!* (Amsterdam: BIS Publishers and Nature Network).

Gilbert, Ian (2013). *Essential Motivation in the Classroom*, 2nd edn (Abingdon and New York: Routledge).

Gilbert, Ian (ed.) (2018). *The Working Class: Poverty, Education and Alternative Voices* (Carmarthen: Independent Thinking Press).

Harris, Michael (2015). *The End of Absence: Reclaiming What We've Lost in a World of Constant Connection* (New York: Current).

Hidalgo, César (2015). *Why Information Grows: The Evolution of Order, from Atoms to Economies* (New York: Basic Books).

Husain, Amir (2018). *The Sentient Machine: The Coming Age of Artificial Intelligence* (London: Sovereign Press).

Jurgenson, Nathan (2019). *The Social Photo: On Photography and Social Media* (New York: Verso).

Kasarda, John and Greg Lindsay (2011). *Aerotropolis: The Way We'll Live Next* (London: Penguin).

Lanier, Jaron (2018). *Ten Arguments for Deleting Your Social Media Accounts Right Now* (London: Bodley Head).

Leader, Darian (2016). *Hands: What We Do with Them and Why* (London: Penguin).

Levy, Joel (2015). *Why We Do the Things We Do* (London: Michael O'Mara Books).

Lucas, Bill and Guy Claxton (2010). *New Kinds of Smart: How the Science of Learnable Intelligence Is Changing Education* (Maidenhead: Open University Press).

Nichols, Tom (2017). *The Death of Expertise: The Campaign Against Established Knowledge and Why It Matters* (New York: Oxford University Press).

Pinker, Steven (2018). *Enlightenment Now: The Case for Reason, Science, Humanism, and Progress* (New York: Viking).

Robinson, Ken with Lou Aronica (2015). *Creative Schools: Revolutionizing Education from the Ground Up* (London: Penguin).

Scott, Laurence (2015). *The Four-Dimensional Human: Ways of Being in the Digital World* (London: Windmill Books).

Taleb, Nassim Nicholas (2018). *Skin in the Game: Hidden Asymmetries in Daily Life* (London: Penguin).

Tegmark, Max (2017). *Life 3.0: Being Human in the Age of Artificial Intelligence* (London: Penguin).

Žižek, Slavoj (2019). *Like a Thief in Broad Daylight: Power in the Era of Post-Humanity* (London: Penguin).

… and a very special mention for this wonderful book – for me, this is as good as it gets!

Berry, Wendell (2018). *The World-Ending Fire* (London: Penguin Books).

I see that paths are not roads (this early morning)

Roads cut through the land – in a hurry to be off somewhere else,

They ignore the left and right of things; so, I step off
and look around,

Searching among the green and gold, for our leafy
ancestral pathways;

Routes, worn clean and furrowed deep in the earth by
our makers.

I have learnt this early morning, as I stepped out along
one such happy path –

That these paths have time for me and show me a
world that is still there

And I have felt this early morning, these past existences
watch and approve.

They are quiet whisperings of what I should always
have understood;

They are willing me on, though the path is new and the
world so changed.

INDEX